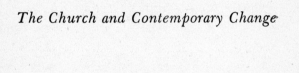

The Church and Contemporary Change

THE MACMILLAN COMPANY
NEW YORK · BOSTON · CHICAGO · DALLAS
ATLANTA · SAN FRANCISCO

MACMILLAN AND CO., LIMITED
LONDON · BOMBAY · CALCUTTA · MADRAS
MELBOURNE

THE MACMILLAN COMPANY
OF CANADA, LIMITED
TORONTO

THE CHURCH
and
CONTEMPORARY
CHANGE

BY

G. Bromley Oxnam

THE MACMILLAN COMPANY

New York : 1950

FIRST PRINTING

ACKNOWLEDGMENTS

Grateful acknowledgment is made for the use of the following quoted material:

Anderson House for permission to quote from "The Wingless Victory" by Maxwell Anderson;

The Bobbs-Merrill Company, Inc. for permission to quote from "Communism and the Conscience of the West" by Fulton J. Sheen, copyright 1948, used by special permission of the publishers;

Henry Holt and Company for permission to quote from "Planning for America" by George B. Galloway and Associates;

The International Convention of the Disciples of Christ for permission to quote from "The Separation of Church and State in America" by Dr. Charles Clayton Morrison;

The International Missionary Council for permission to quote from "Religious Liberty: An Inquiry" by M. Searle Bates;

Virgil Markham for permission to reprint from "The Man with the Hoe" and "The Man with a Hope" by Edwin Markham;

The National Catholic Welfare Conference for permission to quote from "No Wall Between God and the Child" by the Most Rev. J. T. McNicholas, O.P., S.T.D., Department of Education, N.C.W.C., Washington, D.C., 1947;

The author and the Paulist Press for permission to quote from "Freedom of Worship" by the Very Rev. Francis J. Connell;

The Twentieth Century Fund for permission to quote from "Goals for America" and from "The Road We Are Traveling, 1914–1942" by Stuart Chase;

Yale University Press for permission to quote from "Religion, Science and Society in the Modern World" by A. D. Lindsay; and from "The British Labor Movement" by R. H. Tawney;

The Department of the Church and Economic Life of the Federal Council of the Churches of Christ in America for permission to quote from the reports of the National Study Conference on the Church and Economic Life;

The Estate of James Oppenheim for "Bread and Roses" from "Songs for the New Age" by this author.

Printed in the United States of America

Introduction

INTERNATIONAL SKIES ARE DARK. STORM CLOUDS, DRIVEN BY the rising winds of selfish nationalism, revolutionary philosophy, reactionary greed, materialism, and sin, are portents of war. Lightning flashes reveal bewildered leaders of the people whose voices are lost in the thunders of confusion. But wise men hear once again from the mountain tops, "Thou shalt have no other gods before me."

In such an hour the Church must lead. The summons must be clear, courageous, convincing. The Church must summon man to his knees. In the silence of the repentance hour, man must hear the Christ speak again, "Follow Me!" To find His Way; and to apply His Truth in complex situations is fraught with difficulty. "Love thy neighbor as thyself!" What does that mean, when our neighbor is a totalitarian dictator? We are children of one Father. How do we express brotherhood in Palestine? "Seek ye first the kingdom of God." Yes. But, in the seeking, what action is demanded in Czechoslovakia?

Economic and international issues cannot be divorced. Structures designed to establish law and order cannot be reared upon foundations of economic injustice. This is to build houses upon the sand. Houses that would stand the storms must be built upon the rock of the moral law. The Church must come to grips with reality. It dare not be the priest of perfectionism, refusing to soil its hands in ministry to the common life. Nor dare it be the preacher of an expediency that refuses to judge all practices by the absolutes of our faith. The Church has the duty of judging concrete proposals by the absolutes of our faith. The Church never pledges itself in perpetuity to less than the ideal; but it may well give support to measures that presently are less than the ideal; provided they express the greatest measure of common agreement presently possible and that they evidence advance toward the ideal. Just as certainly, the Church must oppose unalterably those measures that upon evidence indicate that we are moving away from the ideal.

The Church must deal with economic injustice. It must not think it has solved the problem of contemporary society by summoning men to a holy war against Communism. It must understand the dynamic challenge to our faith that lies in Communism; but it must know that such a challenge cannot be driven back by bayonets. It is a strange shortsightedness that trains our candidates for the ministry in comparative religion, and rightly so, but fails to acquaint our leaders with the philosophies, the social theories, the tactics, the economics of the contemporary challenges to our faith.

The Nazi talked of a "master race." He brazenly conceived a world in which the Nazi would be master and the rest of mankind serfs. The Communist does not talk of a "master race." He talks of a "classless society." He does not envision a serflike mankind, but proclaims he is out for "the abolition of the exploitation of man by man." Invading armies must be met by defending armies, who subsequently take the initiative and destroy the invader; but an invading ideology that appeals to the "exploited" must be met by a better ideology that has demonstrated its ability to bring better life to human beings. Dynamic democracy is a better society than dictatorship can ever build.

The most effective anti-toxin to dictatorship abroad is life-giving democracy at home. It is a healthy democracy that is immune to Communist bacteria. Liberty, equality, and fraternity are contagious, and if present in sufficient vitality may become epidemic. Let people who suffer dictatorship behold a nation in which man has preserved his liberty, established equality, and practices fraternity, and it is as certain as day follows night that such vision will become a revolutionary force that will not rest until freedom is won. Socially controllable inequalities must be removed.

It is less the materialism, the dictatorship, and the economics of Marxism that have attracted masses of men than the promise of more abundant living, the abolition of the exploitation of man by man, and the setting up of a classless society. It is the hope that the masses behold in Communism that hypnotizes them. These goals cannot be attained by the Communist method of class war and the use of dictatorship. They can be won for man in the freedom of democracy.

Communism moves forward with power because its leaders know what they want and believe they know how to get it. They have kindled fires of enthusiasm in the hearts of their youth, and these young people, united in a common cause, become a conflagration sweeping through the forests of exploitation. We reject Communism. We know that within the freedom of democracy we can build a society at once just and brotherly, in which creative talent may be fully evoked and human beings may live in peace and security, enjoying fearless leisure and fruitful labor, and in which the impulse to creative action and service will be stronger than the acquisitive impulse. The Church must recruit youth, acquaint them with the thousand-year struggle for political freedom, fire them with passion to preserve it, and, more, to use it to bring equality and fraternity to their fellows.

We get nowhere by ringing tocsin bells, by digging our underground caverns and making ready for the atomic bombs of Communism. We win the future by moving into the sunlight. Intelligence and a social conscience pledged to enthrone the moral law in social practice, can end poverty, create full employment, release creative powers, direct atomic energy to the enrichment of personality, and, what is of greater importance, give the spirit of man full opportunity to love God with all his mind and soul and strength and his neighbor as himself.

Churchmen acquainted with the centuries know that the struggle to emancipate the worker is part of the agelong resolve to lift man to the status of a brother.

This whole issue is of major concern to the Church. Such terms as "economic order," "the industrial machine," and "economic democracy" must not obscure the fact that we are dealing with human beings. Where human beings are present, the Church must go, because, for the churchman, personality is of infinite worth. Institutions must be tested by their contribution to the enrichment of personality. Just as the State must be regarded as an instrument to be used by the people and for them, so, too, the economic order, with its vast industrial machine, its rich resources of soil, and its technology, must be regarded as a means whereby life shall be made fuller for all, in a word, "abundant," as Jesus put it.

The Church, therefore, calls for the rebasing and the remotivating of the work life to the end that genius may have full opportunity for expression, and men, in the coöperation of full employment, may make the earth productive.

What is needed today is an approach to this whole issue, not in terms of pre-determined dogmatism but in terms of the Christian Gospel, resolving to use scientific means to achieve moral ends. For men to say that we lose our freedom when intelligently we use the best means to express the Christian ideal is ridiculous. Surely the people in democratic decision can determine what is best for the nation, not only in terms of fiscal policy but in terms of the conservation of our natural resources and, what is more important than any of these, the building up of the spiritual resources of the nation. Men are not free when they are bound by the dogmatism of a particular way of realizing an ideal. They are free when they use the best means to give the ideal the fullest expression.

Outposts of the Gospel now take on major significance in a world of warring ideologies. The lines of communication must be kept open. Reinforcements must reach them in increasing numbers. These our brethren who maintain the far-flung lines of the Kingdom must know that the Church has resolved at last to pledge its all in the grand attack that means final victory. Nations, winning their independence, and taking their places at last in the United Nations, are about to make fundamental choices concerning their ways of life. Are these ways to be the ways of materialism, or the way of Christ?

Small minorities of Christians in all lands now are at the place where they may exercise decisive influence. Are the dynamic forces of statism and totalitarianism to conquer, or are these forces to be met by a vital Christian movement, that, refusing disobedience to the heavenly vision, fighting the good fight, keeping the faith, may yet behold a society in which He is indeed King of Kings and Lord of all? These groups must be strengthened, and at once, lest they be overwhelmed.

There is a hunger in the realm of the spirit that can be satisfied only by the bread of life. There is a thirst in the soul never quenched except by living water. There is loneliness of heart across the face of the earth. Who is to bring to the lonely the

[xi]

knowledge of One who said, "Lo, I am with you alway"? There are dispirited who know full well that it is sin from which they must be saved, if they are to be released from bondage. Where are the disciples to repeat His words, "Thy sins are forgiven thee"?

"Greater love hath no man than this, that a man lay down his life for a friend" were words spoken by One who gave His life upon the cross. He also said, "Whatsoever ye shall ask in my name, that will I do." "My peace I give unto you." It is indeed the peace that passeth all understanding.

It is precisely here that the issue of the world mission of the Church must be faced, here at the cross, here in the presence of our Lord.

This volume is based upon the addresses delivered at The Chicago Theological Seminary on the Alden-Tuthill Lectureship, and upon The Earl Lectures delivered at The Pacific School of Religion, Berkeley, California. I desire to record my gratitude to President Arthur Cushman McGiffert, Jr., who was President of The Pacific School of Religion when The Earl Lectures were given and, interestingly enough, had just taken up his work as President of The Chicago Theological Seminary when The Alden-Tuthill Lectures were presented, for the privilege of appearing upon these well-known Foundations, and to both Dr. McGiffert and Mrs. McGiffert for delightful hospitality and the joy of meeting their charming and distinguished friends at Berkeley and Chicago.

G. BROMLEY OXNAM

Contents

I.   The Nature of the Contemporary Crisis .   1

II. The Minister in a New Environment :.) [•] 31

III. Religious Liberty and the Changing World   49

IV. The Social Service State and Serfdom .   . 81

V.   Christian Strategy in the Light of the
     World Crisis 105

[xiii]

ONE

The Nature of the Contemporary Crisis

CONTEMPORARY CHRISTIANS HAVE BEEN CATAPULTED INTO AN era of change. Professor Alfred N. Whitehead insisted that prior to 1914 the expectancy of continuity was greater than the expectancy of change, but that following 1914 the expectancy of change was greater than the expectancy of continuity. If Professor Whitehead were alive today, I think he would point out that the issue is no longer one of change or of continuity, but rather the nature of change. Change is inevitable.

Military men use a term called "the turning movement." During the execution of a turning movement, the units appear to be hopelessly involved. Nevertheless, there is military method in what appears to be military madness. The turning movement results in a change of front. An army may be marching toward the east, but when a turning movement is executed, the army is marching toward the north. The Church has been caught up in one of the great turning movements of history.

The transition now in effect is as significant as was the passage from slavery to feudalism, and from feudalism to capitalism. No man can foresee the future, but all men with eyes to see witness change. In such an hour, scientific means must be discovered and used to realize moral ends. Man must develop a splendid synthesis in which the creative initiative that flowed from individualism is conserved, and the benefits that lie in collective action are appropriated.

The underlying question must be faced. Is it to be the change of consent or the change of coercion? The former involves democracy; the latter may involve dictatorship. In one, reason rules and change is peaceful. In the other, emotion is dominant, and the violence that flows from greed and hate is present. If change is to be the change of consent, there must be agreement in the realm of ends and sufficient agreement for coöperation in the matter of means. It is not enough to proclaim the ideal. The ideal must come alive in the common life and be translated into the realities of world law and order, economic justice, and racial brotherhood. The "good news" must be proclaimed, but the "good news" must become the good life. The change of consent implies the free mind in the free society seeking the truth that frees. The change of coercion may mean the imposition of a way of life upon conquered peoples by an invading army. An ideology may be imposed by a revolutionary group that seizes power when conditions favorable to revolution have developed. In such cases a minority by infiltration and rigorous discipline takes power, sets up dictatorship and establishes the police state.

Dictatorship decapitates its opposition. Democracy dignifies it. In England the opposition is called "His Majesty's opposition." In Russia such opposition as becomes vocal is tortured, forced to confess, and stood up before the firing squad.

In the change of consent, the avenues through which originality may flow are kept open; and the techniques of change are written into the basic law so that adaptation to changing environment may be made by free men in peaceful coöperation.

Political scientists have long stressed the fact that the community has two aspects: one, the collective aspect called "the State"; and, two, the distributive aspect called "Society." Each member of the community, as a citizen, is a part of the larger entity called the State. This is the collective aspect of the community, namely, the State. In a democratic community, the individual belongs to other groups. These groups have their own existence and are distributed through the community. Thus in the distributive aspect of the community we find the church, the labor union, the teachers' association, the chamber of commerce. In each of these distributive groups there is the interplay of ideas and the discussion of interests and of views. These groups, added up, constitute Society. The creative and constructive, as well as at times critical, discussions within these groups, added together, provide the proper checks and balances upon the larger entity called "the State." The dictator fears these distributive groups because he sees in them the centers of popular control. When Hitler came to power, he sought to destroy Society so conceived. He attacked the Church, took over the schools, broke the organizations of labor and of business. He marched the individual into a great crowd, taught him to shout, *"Sieg Heil! Sieg Heil!"* and saw to it that the individual was never again allowed to emerge from the crowd to the freedom of the groups.

Roscoe Pound, former Dean of the Harvard University Law School, pointed out that the fundamental principle of stability is the maintenance of a technique of change. That is, if a state seeks stability, provision for adaptation to changing environment must be made in the governmental system. The governmental form itself must provide for the decision of the people. This is fundamental to the change of consent. When change is based upon coercion, all that is needed is the order of the dictator. The police state imposes the change in accord with the dictate.

If Society is to exercise its proper role, and, through distributive groups, maintain the constructive criticism that forever checks the tendencies within the state to become the tyrant, the creative centers of individualism must be maintained. For instance, the independent editor of an independent paper in a small town spoke his mind. Several independent papers in a city are good for the people. Independence passes, however, when the papers are bought up and owned by one man, or, worse, by a great syndicate. The local man takes orders from the national man. Before long, a great newspaper chain molds the thinking of the people. An editorial that appears in New York appears simultaneously in San Francisco. The interplay of ideas so essential to a dynamic democracy is lost. Dictatorships are never as wise as democracy because constructive criticism is forbidden and the opposition is decapitated. When a democracy reduces the number of independent critics by consolidating its newspapers into a few major combines or its approach to the people through the radio to a few networks, the chief values of a free press or a free radio are jeopardized.

There must be a reversal of the trend toward centralization. We must move back in order to go forward, back to the independent journalist, back to the independent preacher, back to the independent teacher, back to the independent business man, back to the independent labor organization. The real danger of regimentation lies in a people who are becoming a people of big ears and eyes. As a people, we are called upon to listen and to look. There is less time for critical evaluation. Somebody tells the people what to think on the ralio or how to feel in the pictures, and even the pictures we see are sent out with little chance for choice in the local community. The nation needs the voices of free men, the editorials of free writers, the genius of free business men, the creativity of free labor leaders, the leadership of a free church. Big business is turning to the big church to save it from the big threat, blind to the fact that bigness itself may be a destructive force. Technology may demand mass production, but mass production must be democratically controlled if we are to avoid the danger of developing the mass man who, in turn, composes the revolt of the masses. The individual must be brought back into the control of all that affects individuals.

I

There are two fundamental issues in contemporary change that must be faced. They are the issues of power and of justice. Those who believe in change by consent insist, and properly so, that power—all forms of power—must be brought under democratic control. They demand that justice shall be established by the democratic process. The first will involve basic revisions in our conceptions of sovereignty; the second, similar revisions in our conceptions of property. Those who think of change by coercion consider seizing power and using that power to establish their convictions relative to justice.

Power does corrupt; and it will corrupt a bishop as well as a business man, a church as well as a state. Man has found no other way to control power save to vest it in the people themselves. This is another way of affirming the doctrine of consent. Governments do derive their just power from the consent of the governed. Dictatorship is not only destructive of freedom, but a fundamental denial of the dignity of man. The democratic control of power and the establishment of justice by the democratic process are objectives that must be sought simultaneously.

II

Change is occasioned not alone by research and technological advance but by the aspirations of the human spirit. Thus, one of our problems is that of reconciling the necessities of technology and the necessities of brotherhood. The most important single social fact of our time is the yearning of the common man for abundant life, coupled with the common man's conviction that only selfishness and ignorance stand between him and that life.

In years gone by, I saw women hitched to wagons in Hong Kong, China, dragging the wagons up the steep hill. These women had never entered a laboratory nor were they at home in the library, but by a strange system of communication through which ideas reach the mind of the common man everywhere, they had reached the conclusion that such conditions were no longer necessary, and were determined that their children should not live as they had been forced to live. This yearning for more abundant living, linked to the conviction that the dream of the better life is realizable with what we know now, constitutes a social fact of fundamental importance.

Man has always called for abundant living, but for the first time in history, he believes that abundant life for all men can be realized. The intelligent Greek slave knew that if all the bread produced by all the slaves were equitably distributed, there would not be enough to satisfy the hunger of man. Slavery gave way to feudalism. The worker was freer, but not free. He was a serf, attached to the soil, with obligations to his overlord who, in turn, recognized certain duties to the serf. It was during this historic period that a foolish queen suggested cake for hungry masses who were crying for bread. But if all the cake of all the nobility, and all the bread of all the serfs had been served in equal parts, the world would have

[6]

been hungry still. Feudalism gave way to capitalism. The steam-driven machine, the new economic system with its release of creative ability and its reward to the enterprising, brought forth food in greater quantities than man had ever known, but not enough. The problem of production has not been solved, but man now knows how to produce enough to meet the basic needs of humanity. He can provide food, clothing, and shelter for the human family.

True enough, he has not yet learned how to remove the contradiction that lies in his ability to produce and his inability to distribute in a moral or rationally adequate way. Economic nationalism still erects barriers between the nations and an unimpeded world market. The jungle growth of vested interest seriously impairs the efficiency of the industrial machine and of agricultural production. The fluctuation in import demand and in the flow of investment capital disrupts the economies of nations and of peoples. The common man may not be able to discuss economic theory. He may voice his demands in materialistic terminology or in the explosive slogans of rebellion. He may remain inarticulate while the pressure of resentment and frustration rises. He has eyes to see and ears to hear. He is not given to philosophical analysis, but he asks: what do liberty, equality, and fraternity mean for me and for my children? Blind leaders can never lead men who see. Reactionaries who would block all reform by labeling constructive proposals as milestones upon the road to serfdom play into the hands of revolutionaries who, long since, rejected the way of consent and sold their souls to the immoralities of coercion. With each succeeding day the advances of technology that flow from the research possible in the free society, add to the conviction of the people that abundant life is possible. Yearning plus conviction is a social fact of prime importance. The "exploited" are likely to follow the demagogue who summons them to banners bearing the slogan, "the abolition

[7]

of the exploitation of man by man," unless men who believe in freedom are ready with the resolve and the know-how to set up justice within the conditions of freedom as prelude to brotherhood.

Years ago, James Oppenheim watched a parade of strikers in Lawrence, Massachusetts. Upon one of the banners carried by a young woman he noted the words, "We want bread, and roses too!" He wrote:

As we come marching, marching, in the beauty of the day,
A million darkened kitchens, a thousand mill-lofts gray
Are touched with all the radiance that a sudden sun discloses,
For the people hear us singing, "Bread and Roses, Bread and
    Roses."

As we come marching, marching, we battle, too, for men—
For they are women's children and we mother them again.
Our lives shall not be sweated from birth until life closes—
Hearts starve as well as bodies: Give us Bread, but give us Roses!

As we come marching, marching, unnumbered women dead
Go crying through our singing their ancient song of Bread;
Small art and love and beauty their drudging spirits knew—
Yes, it is bread we fight for—but we fight for Roses, too.

As we come marching, marching, we bring the Greater Days—
The rising of the women means the rising of the race—
No more the drudge and idler—ten that toil where one reposes—
But a sharing of life's glories: Bread and Roses, Bread and Roses!

III

The world crisis is characterized by change. The issues of power and of justice are involved in change, whether of consent or coercion. Technology and the resolve to live abundantly contribute to the underlying trends of the crisis, namely, the trend from selfish nationalism to sensible internationalism, from competitive struggle to coöperative endeavor, from a religion based on authority to a religion grounded in experience.

The conviction is growing that a nationalism that summons sons to war every generation must be brought under law to the end that sons and daughters may make their creative contributions to mankind in peace. Men are realizing that struggle for markets and raw materials is often the real cause of conflict rather than the issues so often stated in idealistic terms. The Japanese who marched into Manchuria were told that they were out to defend democracy. Fathers and mothers whose sons sleep beneath white crosses in foreign fields slowly but surely move to the conclusion that selfish nationalism must give way to sensible internationalism. They deny the validity of theories predicated upon the inevitability of a war of the classes. The people are wondering why competitive struggle rather than coöperative endeavor must characterize the economic life. The experience of the love of God has deepened the desire for the expression of love and goodwill in the process of production so that it may be a coöperative experience. Authoritarianism in religion seems a contradiction in terms. True authority lies in their own experience of Christ's redeeming love, not in the dictates of church or creed or council.

IV

But back of the question of change, the issues of power and of justice, the fundamental fact of the demand for abundant living, and the conviction such life is possible, and more significant than the trends of the period is the basic question of the nature of man.

[9]

Hitler said, "To the Christian doctrine of the infinite significance of the individual, I oppose with icy clarity the saving doctrine of the nothingness of the individual."

I heard Hitler deliver his defense in the German Reichstag for the killings of June 30th and July 1st, 1934. That night the elite of Germany were present. Goering sat in the presiding officer's box. The Fuehrer stood at the rostrum. He said that he took full responsibility for the execution of seventy-seven persons. He informed us that when the state was in danger he was the state. He had lied in each instance. The minimum estimate of the killed was 1,200. Some believed 5,000 were killed that evening. Certain it is his opposition for a time was decapitated. I did not know what he meant by the phrase, "the nothingness of the individual." Later I was to learn. Soon after our forces took Weimar I visited the terrible concentration camp at Buchenwald. Here 52,000 had died. As I looked upon these people still wearing the prison uniform, many hardly able to stand, it seemed that I was in a terrible dream. One who looks upon many faces in an audience knows that the contour of the human face is that of an oval. When I looked upon these people I realized something was wrong, grotesquely wrong. Suddenly I saw. The contour was not that of an oval but of a triangle. These people, starved, with cheeks sunken, foreheads protruding, pointed chins, were looking at me through burning eyes and out of a triangular face. "The nothingness of the individual."

Mussolini, in characteristic bombast, shouted, "Let's have done with this talk of brotherhood. The relations of states are the relations of force. One cry has come down upon the waves of the centuries and the series of generations, 'Woe to the weak.' " No wonder he could write in his classic definition of Fascism that "Fascism is for the individual insofar as he coincides with the State. For Fascism, the State is absolute before which individuals and groups are relative." Later they were to hang him up by his feet like a pig in the city of Milan, but for a time he stood as a Caesar, enunciating a doctrine of man that drove the Fascist forces at first to conquest and then to defeat. Stalin gives his strength to a philosophy of materialism and a theory of social development that flows from it. Man is seen as but an incident in an inexorable historical process. Slave labor and the terrible prison camps are the logical result of such a concept of man.

Jesus of Nazareth believed that every individual is created by the Eternal and in His Image, a being of infinite worth. He held that each human being is a self-conscious personality, capable of distinguishing right and wrong, morally responsible, immortal. For Him, personality was the supreme good and He tested institutions by their effect upon personality. Even the most sacred of institutions was judged by this test. The Sabbath was made for man, not man for the Sabbath.

Is man a being of infinite worth, of such value that the Eternal out of love sends His Son to reveal that love to man and thus to redeem him? As a son of the Father of us all, man belongs to one family, and all members are brothers. The Christian doctrine of the dignity of man roots in the love of God. It flowers in the affirmation that man is of infinite worth. The rights of man derived from the love of God belong to man absolutely because he is the son of God. The State does not confer such rights, it merely confirms them. They are inalienable. Man is endowed with them. They inhere in the fact of his manhood.

In the crisis the common man seeks, as blind men seek for light, a doctrine of the nature of man that will give him a sense of inestimable worth and that will inspire him to build a society worthy of such a being.

V

Some years ago, when it was my honor to serve as President of DePauw University, among the lecturers of a certain year was the Grand Duchess Marie of Russia. She told the story of her life as a princess. Following the lecture we had a supper at our home and invited twenty of the women students in to meet the Grand Duchess. During the course of the evening, because I had but recently read her book called, "The Education of a Princess," I said, "I do not see how you could have written that book." I had in mind the fact that her relatives had been executed and assassinated and that she herself had escaped almost miraculously. She said, "I do not understand what you mean." I replied, "I am a little fearful if I had gone through such experiences and could write about them, my book would reveal resentment; in fact, it might manifest a touch of hatred." She thought for a moment and then replied quietly and I think profoundly. She said, "You do not hate an earthquake, do you?"

That is exactly what had happened in Russia. It was an earthquake. Just as there are physical fault-lines in the earth's crust and along these lines come the tears and the rips that mean earthquake in earthquake territory, so too, there are fault-lines in the social crust, fault-lines of injustice and of exploitation, and along these lines come the tears and the rips that mean social earthquake. Physical fault-lines cannot be removed. All that can be done is to build earthquake resisting buildings. Fortunately, social fault-lines can be removed. The leadership of Russia was unintelligent. It did not remove the fault-lines. In 1905 the nation felt the first tremors of earthquake shock. In 1917 came the terrific seismic disturbance that brought the social structure to ruin. There were three fundamental causes that led to the Russian revolution. First, the autocracy of the czarist system. In the trying days before the abdication, the Czarina wrote to the Czar, urging him to be strong, saying, "Russia loves to feel the whip." Loving it or not, the people had felt it for many weary centuries. The way to Siberia was in fact a "well-worn road with snows incarnadined" and its tortured travelers possessed little save the "worn sandals of a tireless faith." Russia has had a thousand years of bloodshed. With the beginning of the nineteenth century, the people demanded change. The first insurrections were led by army officers who were determined to rid Russia of czarist despotism. Repression was met by attempted revolution. Alexander II was assassinated. Alexander III ruled with an iron hand. Today his hated statue stands in the square opposite the railroad station in Leningrad and upon it has been carved a verse of Demian Byedny:

THE SCARECROW

My son and my father were executed when living
And now disgrace has overtaken me even after death;
I stand here like a brazen scarecrow for the land
That has shaken off forever the yoke of autocracy.

How strange these words sound now when the reader confronts the fact of a new autocracy, equally ruthless and contemplating the rule of all mankind! But the autocracy of those days could have been removed by intelligent men, had they possessed the requisite will and vision. In 1926 I visited the cells in the Peter and Paul Prison where men and women who had but called for the democracy we take for granted were imprisoned. Our own poet, Thomas Bailey Aldrich wrote:

From yonder gilded minaret
Beside the steel-blue Neva set,
I faintly catch, from time to time,
The sweet, aerial midnight chime—
    "God save the Tsar!"

[13]

Above the ravelins and the moats
Of the white citadel it floats;
And men in dungeons far beneath
Listen, and pray, and gnash their teeth—
     "God save the Tsar!"

The soft reiterations sweep
Across the horror of their sleep,
As if some demon in his glee
Were mocking at their misery—
     "God save the Tsar!"

In his Red Place over there,
Wakeful, he needs must hear the prayer.
How can it drown the broken cries
Wrung from his children's agonies?—
     "God save the Tsar!"

Father they called him from of old—
Batuschka! . . . How his heart is cold!
Wait till a million scourgèd men
Rise in their awful might, and then—
     "God save the Tsar!"

A second fault-line was the nature of the industrial system
that had developed in Russia in which the owning class was
weak politically; the working class was exploited, highly con-
gested, easily organized, became class-conscious, and after a
time grew to think of itself as the voice of the inarticulate
peasant and the vanguard of revolution. Many do not know
that Russia, while primarily a great agricultural nation, nevertheless developed industrially with unusual rapidity during
the closing decades of the last century and prior to the First
World War. Between 1885 and 1897 the town population increased 33.8%. The population of the entire country increased

in that period but 15.2%. Between 1895 and 1900, the cast
iron production of Great Britain increased 13%, of France,
58%, of Germany, 61%, of the United States, 76%, of Russia,
220%. Of course this precentage gain was upon a small base
but nonetheless significant. During the last five years of the
nineteenth century, Russia averaged annually an increase of
2,812 versts in its railway mileage. A verst is approximately
two-thirds of a mile. Germany, even during the period of most
rapid railway extension averaged but 1,500 kilometers. A kilo-
meter is approximately the same distance as a verst. In 1914,
the United States had three times the number of industrial
operatives to be found in Russia. But there were fewer operatives in large factories. In that year, there were 1,255,000
workers in factories employing 1,000 or more in the United
States; in Russia there were 1,300,000 not including miners.
Forty-three and eight-tenths per cent of the Russian workers
were employed in big factories, but 20.5% of the American
workers at that time labored in large establishments. There
were more workers in factories employing 5,000 or more in
Russia than in industrial Germany. This industrial group,
class-conscious, exploited and organized, became a fertile field
for the revolutionary propaganda of direct action. It used its
industrial power to secure political change as well as industrial
concessions. If the figure 100 is used to indicate the number
of strikes in Russia between 1900 and 1910, the figure of the
same period in the United States would be 35 and in Germany
17. Here was a situation in the nature of a fault-line. It could
have been changed. It was not.

The third cause was the land-hunger of the peasant. Despite
emancipation, serfdom was practically reëstablished in a new
form as a result of economic pressure which resulted from the
necessity of paying taxes and redemption fees; lack of sufficient
land; and certain other legalistic and administrative measures,
such as collective responsibility in the matter of taxes and the

passport system. It was impossible for the "emancipated" peasant to support himself upon the newly acquired land and at the same time to pay the taxes. The landlord found it possible to secure peasant labor in payment of taxes and to buy in abandoned holdings, thereby increasing his estate.

With the coming of the First World War, revolution was submerged in wartime patriotism. Millions were mobilized. As early as 1915, the morale of the army began to break. More than a million men deserted before 1915 had passed into history. Corruption and graft stalked behind the lines; some of the resentment broke into flaming rebellion in the trenches, while from the villages arose a cry, at first like distant thunder, but later like the terrific crash of heavy guns, "Peace! Bread! Land!" The Czar abdicated. There was an attempt to put his brother upon the throne. This failed and a provisional government was established. It maintained power for a short period, then fell. It was followed by the Kerensky regime. Finally, a highly disciplined, revolutionary minority seized power. Rulers bent upon maintaining their privilege had refused the reform essential to better living. Revolution came and with it the ideology that is Communism.

VI

Distinction must be drawn between Russia as an imperialist state and Russia as a Communist society. The former involves an expansionist program, the latter, infiltration and the eventual seizure of power. Measures necessary to block an expanding nation may not prove effective in containing Communism. Military leaders may look with favor upon alliances with reactionary regimes because such regimes may furnish manpower or make available air or other bases, but such alliances may alienate the masses exploited by such regimes and thereby make them the allies of Russia on ideological grounds. To salute Franco to stop Stalin is sheer stupidity. There is no base in Spain as valuable as the goodwill of the British and French worker. Wisdom dictates the maintenance of sufficient military strength to forestall all Communist attempts to impose its ideology by force, as well as to coöperate in repelling the invasion of free countries by Russia; but a national policy based upon an attempt to meet Russian moves by counter moves leaves initiative in Russian hands and in its assumption that revolution in Russia may remove the present regime appears more naïve than realistic. It is true that invading armies must be met by force and be destroyed, but the danger is less that of armed invasion than of ideological infiltration. Ideologies cannot be bombed out of the heads of men; they can be dislodged only by better ideologies. Christianity is an ideology. Its ideology is incarnate in a person. Its proclamation and practice lifts persons to a place of prime consideration. Because the Christian ideal is essentially a person, the Christian is one who, in complete surrender, has given himself to this Person, Who is the Way, the Truth and the Life. But it is more than surrender because the Person summons the follower to action. In social terms, the action calls upon all to build, "a coöperative social order in which the sacredness of every life is recognized and everyone finds opportunity for the fullest self-expression of which he is capable; in which each individual gives himself gladly and wholeheartedly for ends that are socially valuable; in which the impulses to service and to creative action are stronger than the acquisitive impulses, and all work is seen in terms of its spiritual significance as making possible fullness of life for all men; in which differences of talents and capacity mean proportional responsibilities and ministry to the common good; in which all lesser differences of race, of nation, and of class serve to minister to the richness of an all-inclusive brotherhood; in which there hovers over all a sense of the reality of the Christlike God, so that worship inspires service, as service expresses brother-hood."

In individual terms it involves constant association with the Person, and thus with the Father, until at last the purpose and the power, the spirit and the service that characterized Him, rule in the individual. It is an ideology that is alive. It is a love so amazing, so divine, that it demands all.

The Christian ideology is today confronted by Communism. Communism finds the root of evil to lie in property relations. It believes that fundamental adjustments in the realm of property will bring justice, abolish exploitation, and out of it all will emerge the classless society. Christianity's thought is deeper. It recognizes fully the problems that are involved in un-just and unrighteous property relations but knows that there is sin in the human heart. It was stated at Amsterdam, "Men are often disillusioned by finding the changes of particular systems do not bring unqualified good, but fresh evils. New temptations to greed and power arise even in systems more just than those they have replaced, because sin is ever present in the human heart. Many, therefore, lapse into apathy, ir-responsibility and despair. Faith leaves no room for such de-spair, being based on the fact that the Kingdom of God firmly established in Christ and will come by God's act despite all human failure."

VII

In Monsignor Fulton J. Sheen's study of Communism en-titled, "Communism and the Conscience of the West," he says:

The Church is never a true influence in society when the world regards it as a morale builder, whose business it is to rubber-stamp the policies of a party in power. For the sake of clarity a word ought to be said why the Church is *not* opposed to communism.

It is not opposed to communism because communism is anti-capitalistic. If by capitalism is meant, not diffused ownership of property, but monopolistic capitalism in which capital bids for labor on a market, and concentrates wealth in the hands of the few, then from an *economic point of view alone,* the Church is just as much opposed to capitalism as it is to communism. Communism emphasizes social use to the exclusion of personal rights, and capitalism emphasizes personal rights to the exclusion of social use. The Church says both are wrong, for though the right to property is personal, the use is social. It therefore refuses to maintain capitalism as an alternative to the economic side of communism. Monopolistic capitalism concentrates wealth in the hands of a few capitalists, and communism in the hands of a few bureaucrats, and both end in the proletarianization of the masses. The true Christian must rid himself of the delusion that in opposing communism the Church thereby puts itself in opposition to all those who would seek thus to change the present economic system. The Christian concept denies there is an absolutely owned private property exclusive of limits set by the common good of the community and responsibility to the community. The more anonymous and impersonalistic property becomes, the less is the right to it. The Church agrees with communism in its protest against injustice of the economic order, but it parts with it in the collectivity being made the sole employer, for this reduces the individual to the status of serf or a slave of the state. Concentration of wealth is wrong whether it is done on the Hudson or the Volga.

There is a closer relation between communism and monopolistic capitalism than most minds suspect. They are agreed on the materialistic basis of civilization; they disagree only on who shall control that basis, capitalists or bureaucrats. . . . Capitalistic economy is godless; communism makes economics God. . . . It is so easy for those who have made their money under a given system to think that that system must be right and good. . . . The Church, however, knows that the disorganization of the world is largely due to the fact that it is not organized by any conscious acceptance of purpose other than the immediate interest of a capitalistic class on one hand, or a Communist class on the other hand. That is why the economic policy of the Church is consistently in opposition to both capitalism and communism. . . .

There is not a single Russian idea in the whole philosophy of communism. It is bourgeois, Western, materialistic and capitalistic in origin.

Monsignor Sheen saw as did the leaders at Amsterdam that the Christian Gospel is not to be identified with any economic system. Christians in Socialist Britain, Christians in Communist Russia, Christians in Scandinavian countries where coöperatives have been significantly developed, and Christians in capitalist United States, who seek to identify the current economic system with the Christian faith, make the Church but a chaplain to the status quo and deny it the true function of being the teacher of the principles of conduct, a voice of judgment, and the herald of a new day. Furthermore, they miss the fundamental tensions that lie in the realm of faith. The real tension is related to the doctrine of man held by Christians as contrasted to that held by Communists.

In its important statement on American-Soviet relations, the Federal Council of the Churches of Christ in America came to grips with basic issues beyond the ken of little people whose inadequate training in economics results in the proclamation of economic platitudes and whose shocking unfamiliarity with Christian thought results in pagan pronouncements. The Federal Council said:

It is the Christian faith that God's righteous rule is over all men and nations, that in Christ He confronts us all alike in judgment and mercy; that men, though sinful, are made in His image and are not only the concern of His saving work but His agents as well, each of value in His sight without distinction of class, race or condition; that the Church, the body of Christ and the fellowship of Christ's followers, is the creation of His Spirit, and the steward of His purpose; that His Kingdom on earth is an unconquerable

Kingdom of justice and mercy and truth in which it is our responsibility to bring human laws and human institutions into increasing accord with His holy will. . . . Our dedication, therefore, is to the progressive realization of the dignity and worth of man in every area of life—political, economic, social and religious —to the world-wide achievement of man's individual freedom, under God, to think, to believe, and to act responsibly according to the dictates of his own conscience. This, we believe, is indispensable if God's will for man is to be fulfilled. . . . Within the Soviet Union there are many people who share such Christian beliefs. Moreover, communism as an economic program for social reconstruction has points of contact with the social message of Christianity as in its avowed concern for the underprivileged and its insistence on racial equality. However, Marxist communism in its orthodox philosophy stands clearly opposed to Christianity. It is atheistic in its conception of ultimate reality and materialistic in its view of man and his destiny. Its utopian philosophy of history lacks the essential Christian notes of divine judgment, divine governance, and eternal victory. Its revolutionary strategy involves the disregard of the sacredness of personality which is fundamental in Christianity.

The World Council of Churches at Amsterdam saw the issue clearly and whole. It said:

The points of conflict between Christianity and the atheistic Marxian communism of our day are as follows: (1) the communist promise of what amounts to a complete redemption of man in history; (2) the belief that a particular class by virtue of its role as a bearer of a new order is free from the sins and ambiguities that Christians believe to be characteristic of all human existence; (3) the materialistic and deterministic teachings, however they may be qualified, that are incompatible with belief in God and with the Christian view of man as a person, made in God's image and responsible to Him; (4) the ruthless methods of communists in dealing with their opponents; (5) the demand of the party on its members for an exclusive and unqualified loyalty which belongs only to

[21]

God, and the coercive policies of communist dictatorship in controlling every aspect of life.

Amsterdam made it abundantly clear that the Church is utterly opposed to "all forms of tyranny, economic, political or religious, which deny liberty to men." Amsterdam said, "We utterly oppose totalitarianism, wherever found, in which a state arrogates to itself the right of determining men's thoughts and actions instead of recognizing the rights of each individual to do God's will according to his conscience."

Amsterdam also said:

The Church should make clear that there are conflicts between Christianity and capitalism. The developments of capitalism vary from country to country and often the exploitation of the workers that was characteristic of early capitalism has been corrected in considerable measure by the influence of trade unions, social legislation and responsible management. But (1) capitalism tends to subordinate what should be the primary task of any economy—the meeting of human needs—to the economic advantages of those who have most power over its institutions. (2) It tends to produce serious inequalities. (3) It has developed a practical form of materialism in western nations in spite of their Christian background, for it has placed the greatest emphasis upon success in making money. (4) It has also kept the people of capitalist countries subject to a kind of fate which has taken the form of such social catastrophes as mass unemployment.

The Christian churches should reject the ideologies of both communism and laissez-faire capitalism, and should seek to draw men away from the false assumption that these extremes are the only alternatives. Each has made promises which it could not redeem. Communist ideology puts the emphasis upon economic justice, and promises that freedom will come automatically after the completion of the revolution. Capitalism puts the emphasis upon freedom, and promises that justice will follow as a by-product of free enterprise; that, too, is an ideology which has been proved false. It is the responsibility of Christians to seek new, creative solutions which never allow either justice or freedom to destroy the other.

Too many think of Communism as merely an economic system. Actually it is a philosophy of history, a consistent and coherent creed composed of principles that rule all the activities of man and control the state. It is also a theory of social development as well as an economic theory. Communism is also a carefully planned system of tactics by which the overall strategy is to be carried out. Religion is in tension with Communism in each of these aspects, since in Communist philosophy it is held that the prevailing mode of production is decisive in the determination of social institutions, culture, morals, and that ultimate reality is material; since in Communist social theory the owners of the instruments of production use the state as a tool for their further exploitation of the worker thus accentuating the differences of the classes until class war itself becomes the rule; since in its economic theory private property becomes a monopoly of capital and the centralization of the means of production and socialization of labor reach a point where they become incompatible with their capitalist integument and may burst asunder; and since in its tactics it relies upon the war method, dictatorship, the crushing out of opposition and the suppression of individual freedom.

Christians are apt to dismiss Communism as materialistic. Nicolas Berdyaev, who had eyes to see and ears to hear, wrote, "The question of bread for myself is a material question, but the question of bread for my neighbors, for everybody, is a spiritual and a religious question." The Communist rules out absolute concepts. He insists that such terms as freedom, justice, and brotherhood have no reality in themselves. The Communist sees society as persons in relation—this is substance, reality. John MacMurray in his "Philosophy of Com-

[23]

munism" makes it clear that for the Communist the term capital is an abstraction. The reality is the person who lives by owning property. Labor is an abstraction. The reality is the person who lives by selling his labor. Therefore, when we speak of capital and labor, we are really speaking of persons in certain relations: namely, the one who can live for a more or less indefinite period because of what he owns and the one who can exist but a few days because unless he can sell his labor he cannot eat. Thus he takes freedom out of abstraction and sees it as freedom to eat or to starve.

The rejection of absolutes, the denial that reality lies in transcendent moral principle, and the refusal to admit the so-called abstract concepts means that Communism rejects a Christian fundamental, namely, that there has been a revelation of reality in Christ. The revelation of the love and the purpose at the heart of the universe, in a word, God's love, God's purpose, God's forgiveness, God Himself is basic in Christianity. Here the tension is fundamental and final, the difference irreconcilable; one or the other must give way, or the tension continues. This revelation of God in Christ, and the redemption that lies therein, is superstition to the Communist, is salvation to the Christian. Communists see redemption in their program, a redemption in which social injustice shall be ended and the classless society established. There is no God who stands in judgment upon all social systems. The Communist sees victory as inevitable; the historic process works for him; he becomes in effect utopian. The Christian finds evil in the present system of property relations, but is not so naïve as to hold that all evil centers there. There is the sinful heart as well as a system of property relations that is alleged to be so designed as to exploit. Remove the exploitation of man by man that lies in the ownership of the means of production and presto, says the Communist, the new society

[24]

is here. Remove exploitation by all means, says the Christian, but recall, too, wrongs that flow from love of power, prestige, display, from passion and greed. The Communist may reject reform as inadequate, may call for revolution as imperative, but misses the essential of regeneration that must reach the heart.

There is an irreconcilable difference between Marxian atheism and Christian theism. But here again we must deal with realities. The Marxist is avowedly an atheist. Christians must be opposed not alone to the philosophical atheism of Communism and the practices that flow from it, but also opposed to the practical atheism of those sections of Capitalism that refuse to admit God's rules or relevance to the economic process. A Communist who supports an atheistic attempt to crush out religion known as the Society of the Godless, is not too far separated from some capitalists who may support a church with gifts but rule God out of the economic process.

It is at the point of the treatment of persons that Christianity and Communism are, and will be, in tension. "Love your enemies" makes no sense to a Communist. On the contrary, his morality demands the destruction of enemies, and the use of any means to destroy. It has been pointed out that acquiescence in inequality, or the calm acceptance of child labor or the high death rate among the poor due to preventable disease, does not differ in essence from the liquidation of kulaks or the use of prison labor. I do not for a moment justify child labor, but to equate morally the apathy that delayed the abolition of child labor, with the deliberate murder of hundreds of thousands of human beings, is to make words meaningless. My brother, who was in charge of the development of copper in certain sections of Russia—he of course being in the employ of an American corporation and deeply resentful of the whole approach to human beings and of the denial of liberty he found in Russia—told me that during the "liquidation" of the kulaks he had seen perhaps 5,000 kulaks dumped out on the plains of Tashkent just before winter, without food, without winter clothes, without habitation, thrown there to die. The Christian conscience spoke in condemnation of child labor and here it is largely gone, but the Communist conscience justified the killing of these people. I once heard a distinguished Christian who had turned, it seemed to me, to Communism, justify such action as a "war measure." No, there is a fundamental difference here, and tension is irreconcilable.

The Christian holds that man is a being of infinite worth. The Communist sees him as an incident in the inexorable historical process. Reality is in that process.

Professor Edward Hallet Carr in "The Soviet Impact Upon the Western World," in his brilliantly written fifth chapter entitled "The Ideological Impact" sees the revolutionary impact of Marxist ideology as lying in (1) Its materialism, (2) Its dialectical character, and (3) Its relativism. He says, "Revolutionary materialism was a revolt both against a metaphysical idealism which believed in spiritual values and pure ideas as the ultimate reality behind the material universe. Translated into political terms, it attacked the privileged classes by alleging their preoccupation with men's souls masked a convenient and profitable neglect of the needs of men's bodies." Thus the Communist evokes from men a fervor similar to that of the Christian evangelists only he is out to improve their material standards rather than to win their souls.

Marx saw the historical process in terms of the conflict not alone of ideas, but of classes. This continuous process of thesis being met by antithesis, and out of the impact synthesis emerging, which in turn becomes the new thesis, was for Marx ultimate reality. Marx really substituted the conflict of classes with their interests grounded in the material for the conflict of ideas. The main point here, and Carr stresses it, is that if one holds that the historic process in never-ending change is reality, then there can be no absolute outside of it. Some say that to assume history is with a man is to reduce his efforts, since he is to win anyhow. This is not true; men like to be on the winning side and work to accelerate the process. We say God's will is to rule, that Christ will become the ruler of the kings of the earth. Some, it is true, sit back, and say irreverently, "Let God do it," but most Christians labor the harder as co-workers with God. Communism tends to justify the means, any means, that accelerate the inevitable victory.

But its relativism brings Communism into continuous tension with Christianity. Communism, as stated earlier, tears such concepts as freedom and justice apart, by asking "freedom for whom, and from what"; "justice for whom and at whose expense." "Reality," Carr says, "is never static; everything is relative to a given stage in the historical process. This thorough-going relativism is ideologically the most destructive weapon in the Marxist armoury. It can be used to dissolve all the absolute ideas on which the existing order seeks to base its moral superiority." But this "relativism" goes "deeper still. If the institutional pattern of society and the ideals which animate it are conditioned by the material—or specifically by the economic—foundations on which the society rests, so also are the thought and action of its individual members. Marxism finally deprived the individual of his individuality and made him, first and foremost, the member of a class. Individualism, having challenged and destroyed the authority of other sources of value and set up the individual judgment as the ultimate source, carries the argument to its logical conclusion and proves this source also is tainted. . . . The reason of the individual can have no independent validity. His thinking is conditioned by his social situation, and that situation is in turn determined by the stage reached in the historical process." This is tantamount to the rejection of all absolute truth.

Beneath all of this lies the vital question: How can individualism be preserved in the mass society? The World Council is giving major attention to the issue of the evangelization of man in a mass society. Communism will find that the problem of humanity will not be solved even if its utopian dream is realized and its so-called absolute attained, namely, the emancipation of the proletariat and the setting up of the classless society.

The tension will continue to center in the issue of theism versus atheism, in the question concerning the nature and the worth of the individual person.

A church confronting Communism must be clear and concrete:

1. Christians of the twentieth century, like their brothers of the first century, must out-think, out-love and out-serve contemporary paganism; in a word, the Christian must out-live the Communist and reveal in his conduct the superiority of his faith.

2. Communism is a consistent and coherent creed, and those who would overcome its atheism and its materialism, must master the affirmations of the Christian faith and thus be able to give a reason for their faith in God and in the reality of the moral law.

3. Christians who bow God out of the economic life and who insist that God's laws are not relevant to the economic order are in fact practical atheists and in no position to condemn the avowed atheism of Communists.

4. The exploitation of one man by another is of greater concern to the Christian theist than to the Communist atheist because the Christian believes every man is of infinite worth,

created by the Eternal and in His image, a child of one Father, a member of one family, a self-conscious personality, capable of distinguishing right and wrong, morally responsible, immortal.

5. Christians must not identify the Gospel with any economic system, Communist, Capitalist, Socialist. The Gospel stands in judgment upon all systems.

6. Communism is an ideology and cannot be demolished by atomic bombs nor suffocated by poison gas. It must be answered by a better ideology that can demonstrate its ability when applied to bring more of liberty, equality and fraternity to mankind.

7. Hysteria and hatred contribute to Communist advance because the hysterical cease to think with clarity and hatred develops the suspicion that divides. At the very moment a united people is necessary as we confront the Communist challenge to freedom, hysterical people of little knowledge and of sadistic spirit seek to lynch their fellow citizens by label, to damn necessary reform by calling it Communist and thereby play into the hands of the Communist who desires the maintenance of injustices and the division of the people by fear and falsehood.

8. A dynamic democracy, in which the ethical ideals of religion are within the conditions of freedom translated into the practices of justice and brotherhood, is impregnable to Communist infiltration.

9. The totalitarian has conquered when a democratic people abrogate their civil liberties and adopt the totalitarian technique to meet the totalitarian threat.

10. A revival of religion, in which the regenerating power of God's love and forgiveness, righteousness and justice, is let loose in the world, and by which the individual heart is changed and our political, social and economic life becomes Christian in spirit and practice, is the most certain way to

contain Communism, to conquer in the name of Christ, and to preserve freedom for our children and our children's children.

VIII

At the center of the crisis is the question of the nature of man. If he is a son of God, a being of infinite worth, if personality is the supreme good, and moral law is written into the nature of things, man must recognize his kinship with men everywhere and pledge himself absolutely to seek until he has discovered the will of God, and upon finding it, to obey it. Since for most men ideas become meaningful when beheld incarnate in other men, the Eternal sent a Son who took upon Himself the limitations of humanity, revealed God's will to men, and in His Person, made manifest the way for humanity, incarnated the truth by which men must live and lived so victoriously Himself that He became the Life.

TWO

The Minister in a New Environment

JOHN FOSTER DULLES IN HIS REMARKABLE VOLUME ENTITLED
"War or Peace" states, "Change is the law of life, of international life as well as national and personal life. If we set
up barriers to all change, we make it certain that there will
be violent and explosive change." Change is also the law of
life in the economic and the social sphere. Environment
therefore changes. The minister in fact is living in a new
world. Those who proclaim the unchanging moral principles
written into the nature of things must be aware of contemporary change if the full message of the Changeless is to be
brought in power to a changing society.

Alexander D. Lindsay, Master of Balliol College, Oxford,
in his Terry Lecture at Yale entitled "Religion, Science, and
Society in the Modern World," says, "The beginning of the
modern adventure in both science and religion was the revival of the essentially Christian conception of the infinity of
God and the consequent realization that God had given man
an infinite task in understanding and doing His will and
knowing His world. This meant the giving up of all formula-

[31]

tions of the will of God which claimed to be final and all intellectual constructions into which new discovery had to be fitted. It meant a belief in experiment and diversity. It meant finally—and this was alike the glory and the danger of the adventure—that the unity which was to keep men together in this many-sided experiment could not be a unity of accepted formulae but the unity of a common life of fellowship." He continues in the penetrating fashion we associate with his writings, "If creation and activity are a fundamental truth of reality, then the teaching of the Hebrew prophets that God is a God of righteousness finds an intellectual framework, and the conception of goodness will itself alter. Moral action will not be the copying or imitation of a changeless pattern—as in a world where changeless patterns are more real than living, changing persons. Morality will be itself creative and growing and developing. If in the classical view the purpose of the state was to formulate, realize and preserve a changeless code, it will be the task of the state according to the new philosophy to find room for and give scope to development and progress."

Christianity holds before us the demands of perfection, but perfection ever eludes us. There is a beckoning quality about the absolute that forever summons man who is determined to reach the ultimate but knows that the ultimate will always be beyond him. Lindsay tells us that many people insist upon setting up a Christian society or a Christian economic system, "but the challenge of Christian perfection implies that that is a vain demand. We are indeed called upon to bring about a better society, a better state, a better economic system, to bring our institutions nearer to the mind of Christ; but if we think we can produce a complete Christian model, we have not understood Christian perfection or the meaning of the Sermon on the Mount."

The proclamation of the moral ideal in itself effects change. The Church teaches the principles of conduct and voices moral judgment. It also heralds a new day. The assumption of some theologians that God Himself will establish His Kingdom and that man is not to consider himself a co-worker in that endeavor puts the Christian at serious disadvantage when confronted by a Communist who is determined to set up a classless society. The Communist is also bound to an assumption that there is an inexorable process at work and that out of this process the Communist society inevitably emerges, but he finds in his doctrine a summons to use all his powers to accelerate the historical process. If a minister prays, "Thy Kingdom come," and placidly sits in the fig-tree shade to await its coming, he is likely to find himself alone because men will have marched past him, carrying banners that proclaim, "Faith without works is dead." The minister must follow Jesus into contemporary society, carrying his convictions and possessed of his courage, determined to enthrone his ideals.

Reconnaissance is a military essential. Those who face the world, the flesh and the devil, or in modern terms the impact of atheistic Communism, pagan fascism, and, unfortunately, in some areas of capitalism an insistence that God is irrelevant to the economic process must likewise learn to reconnoiter.

I

The minister must distinguish between the spent forces about to relinquish power and dynamic forces about to assume power. He witnesses the emergence of a new world of labor in which the worker wins new status, new power, new responsibility. He beholds the coming of the social service state and notes that increasing numbers of people believe that the state democratically controlled can become an instrument of service. He sees also a new world of law and order emerging. It will mark the end of international anarchy. Sovereignties of nations will bow to the higher sovereignty of the world to the end that justice may be established and peace may endure. He notes the trend that will mark the passing of competitive struggle in the coming of coöperative endeavor. In the society that is passing, the driving force has been the pursuit of self-interest; the chief rewards have gone to the owners of the means of production; inequality was accepted as inevitable but lessened somewhat by charity; the possessors of property too often looked upon the state as a tool to be used by them and for them; and the underlying philosophy was material-istic. Charity was at times a matter of cold calculation; at other times a true expression of love and therefore really beneficent.

There were some who really thought they could establish a corporation known as God, Mammon and Company. Mammon himself proved to be of passable morality in polite society. The community was stricter in matters of personal violation of the moral law than of its social violation. It pinned a scarlet letter upon an adulteress, but considered it a red-letter day when a person of wealth joined the church. It did not ask if his five-, ten-, and fifteen-cent stores with their low wages contributed to prostitution. Morality was in a confused state. The Valjeans who stole bread were punished, but there was little comment concerning the powerful who devoured widows' houses. Personal morality was a matter of religion; social morality was nobody's business. Some men saw danger in the measures of social security but marched without fear in political processions that demanded high tariffs. Govern-ment was of course of the people, by the people, and for the people, but after all they must be *the* people. Accompanying the philosophy of materialism was the acceptance of autoc-racy as the organizing principle in the economic life. The basic motivation was greed rather than service. Men who could see that a nation cannot exist half slave and half free did not see that an economic order based upon concepts of democracy in the political sphere but maintaining an autocrat-ically controlled system of production is a house divided against itself.

[34]

In the society that is emerging, the common good will be supreme. This does not mean that the many will overwhelm the one but does mean that the one will find opportunity for the fullest self-expression of which he is capable as he dedicates his talent to the common good and finds himself in the complete gift of self to others. Reward will be based upon service to the group and greatness thus pass, as Jesus predicted, to the servant—the engineer who flings a bridge across the Golden Gate, the researcher who destroys cancer, the teacher who brings the glory of the lighted mind to succeeding generations of students, the genius in organization who makes two blades of grass grow where one grew before, or who causes the desert to bloom as the rose, the man of wisdom who governs the state! The necessities will be provided socially and all socially controllable inequalities will be removed. Intelligent planning in freedom will strive for security, rights will be balanced by duties, among them the universal obligation to work; and underlying all will be the concept that personality is of infinite worth. Intelligent planning striving at once for security and for freedom will supplant unintelligent depletion of natural resources and the greedy pursuit of special privilege. Selfishness never thinks of the generations to come nor of the children of tomorrow. Fundamental to the good society is the fact of freedom. Liberty must be preserved, but it must be used to establish equality and thereby open the way to fraternity.

There is always danger that the minister, facing a changed or changing environment, may become so enamored of the ideals voiced by those who advocate change that he fails to evaluate critically the proposals presented to effect change. He may idealize a labor union or the Socialist party. He may sell his parson's birthright for the partisan's mess of pottage. The values of an order under attack may be obscured by the dust of battle. The minister dare not live in an ivory tower nor resort to the monastery cell, but he must be careful lest he find greater satisfaction in storming barricades than in saving society.

The passing of an economic order too largely that of Mammon does not guarantee that the new society will be that of God. In all probability it will mean that expressions of religion will be less institutional in character, less dependent upon the goodwill and the charity of the chief beneficiaries of the passing order. The minister may have more to do with the discovery and support of measures that give effect to justice and that, accepted by the people, will be by them supported. We may witness the end of the era of great fortunes. If this be so, there should be recorded in the book of history the Christian stewardship of great and wealthy laymen who have regarded their possessions as a sacred trust. It is to be doubted that wealth was ever spent to greater social advantage than by John D. Rockefeller, Jr. Munificent gifts have been made to creative endeavor in the fields of religion, education, medicine, government. Wherever Rockefeller money has gone, life has been enriched. The frontiers of knowledge have been pushed back, and men creatively and coöperatively within the conditions of freedom have moved forward in life-giving service. Men of lesser means but with his spirit have given their millions. Edward Rector gave a fortune to DePauw University. He endowed a scholarship foundation that has opened the doors of opportunity to hundreds of young men. Such men stand as a final contradiction of the Communist caricature in which the American capitalist has been protrayed as ruthless and inhuman. Leaders in education, in religion and in social service are fortunate beyond expression to possess the friendship and the interest of such sincere Christians—men and women of goodwill who sincerely express their religion in giving at once intelligent and generous.

But there has been another side to this picture. There have been those, and unfortunately they have been in the majority, who have never considered wealth a trust. They assumed that it was their due because they assumed that they were people of superior genius. Many college presidents have developed a bedside manner of their own as they have sought annuities and wills. They have become expert in the fawning flattery that "says it with roses" unaware that the devil demands a bit of soul with each bouquet until at last the soul of the solicitor is lost in the endeavor to convince the contributor. If the president is successful, another structure is reared "to the glory of God." This is a form of prostitution and its passing will be without mourning.

II

It is a function of the Church to create the mood requisite to creative change and the spirit essential to the peaceful setting up of justice. Among the first of the services of the Church, after the proclamation of the message of redemption, is the creation of conditions conducive to reconciliation. The regenerating power of religion cannot be brought to men who face each other upon the battlefield. It can be received by those who have been reconciled and who as brothers kneel at an altar before they attempt discussion at the conference table.

The minister must believe implicitly in the faith he proclaims. If he secretly holds that the teachings of Jesus are but perfectionist ethics he is valueless in the changing world.

In his play, "The Wingless Victory," Maxwell Anderson has written a tragedy that, strangely enough, may be called beautiful. It is phrased in the strong, simple English of Elizabethan days, and speaks of the terrible nemesis that forever pursues intolerance. The scene is laid in Salem, Massachusetts, about the year 1800. Nathaniel McQueston and his wife Oparre are the central characters. He is a sea captain who left Salem in poverty to return in wealth. Oparre is a Malay princess, who had saved his life. They return with their two children, to meet the bitter rebuff of racial prejudice, a rebuff in this instance made the more bitter by the covetous spirit of the self-righteous who envied his possessions.

Oparre, once a worshipper of the tribal gods of revenge and blood, is drawn to the gentle, kindly Christ. She seeks to win the love of her husband's people; but they are cruel in their intolerance, even though, in pleading declaration, they hear her say:

> Still carrying in my heart the secret Christ
> by whom you live, I answer, I am your friend.

But she warns them:

> Dark,
> as your words have been, dark as your looks at me,
> evil as you may think you are, your evil
> is as the play of children to the world
> we two have left behind.

But they will have none of her, nor her children. They would ruin her husband. At last she speaks to her husband's brother, a clergyman, whose prejudice is the more terrible because of the very passion of religion:

> Sir, if this winter coast
> is tarnished by our footsteps in the snow,
> as I feared it might be; if the Christ you worship
> gives sanctuary only to his own
> lest they be polluted, say this at once, and we
> shall rouse the children, and be away. I came
> only with a hope.

They have their way with her, and in a moment of awful trial her husband falters, broken by the overwhelming pressure of the community. Knowing that she must leave, and leave alone save for her children and a faithful servant, she repudiates the Christ, rejects all, and turns once again to gods of earth and blood. She boards the ship, resolved to die and take her little ones with her. She speaks of "unwanted babes" and of the "drink of darkness." Taking the poison, with broken heart we hear her say, "We shall sleep and turn back to nameless ground." Awaiting the end, she kneels to utter a prayer—her last. It is addressed to the gods she knew.

> The earth rolls toward the dark,
> and men begin to sleep. God of the children,
> god of the lesser children of the earth,
> the black, the unclean, the vengeful, you are mine
> now as when I was a child. He came too soon,
> this Christ of peace. Men are not ready yet.
> Another hundred thousand years they must drink
> your potion of tears and blood. . . .

"He came too soon, this Christ of peace. Men are not ready yet. Another hundred thousand years . . ." "He came too soon, this Christ."

Many who bow in prayer upon entrance to the church, and not a few who stand in the pulpit itself, carry secret doubts in their minds and hearts concerning the practicability of the teachings of Jesus. There are those who insist that our biological heritage is too strong, that Christ came too soon for men to love one another. It is true that the common people heard Him gladly but it is also true that he was despised and rejected. Nature is red in tooth and claw, we are told. The strong do survive because they are fit. The fit become the elite, destined to rule. Christ came too soon, it is said. Men are not ready yet. He came too soon to present religion as a cup of cold water, to summon men to walk the second mile, to give a cloak when a coat is demanded. He came too soon for Mary of the streets to become Mary of the saints. We have our puritanical codes and we fling the first stone and the last stone. The fighting way of life in which man has lived from the beginning when a brother slew a brother to the present when millions in Christian nations fling their millions against other Christian nations has so conditioned man to struggle

[39]

that he is unready for the Christian command, "Follow me." The fighting way of life has been paralleled by the money-making way of life. The prehensile hand has become the symbol of too much of man's activities. Jesus came too soon, it is argued.

The early Church was ready for the Christ of empire. When the wealth of Constantine came to the Church and leaders began to think of property and power and prestige it was not long before the sword was raised in the form of a cross and men marched under banners, "By this sign conquer." They were ready for the Christ of empire but they were unready for the Galilean Who had no place to lay His head. They were ready for the Christ of dogma, and the medieval theologians debated the niceties of theological statement. They were ready for that, but not for the Christ Who said, "I am the Way, the Truth, and the Life."

In a changing environment a minister alert to change must be loyal to the fundamental principles of the faith. He must call for the rebasing and the remotivating of society in terms of the ethical principles that lie at the heart of his faith, but he must never forget that in an hour of changing environment the central message of Christianity is one of salvation. It was out of love that God sent his Son that those who believe upon Him are saved. All social change in which the minister labors has as its final objective the salvation of the human soul, the reconciliation of man with man, and man with God. The minister rightly calls for the righteousness that must flow down as a mighty stream and insists that Jehovah requires of all men that they do justly, love mercy and walk humbly with their God. He reaffirms the test of the final judgment and declares, "Inasmuch as ye have done it unto one of the least of these ye have done it unto Me." He preaches "the sacred and imperishable message of eternal salvation" that men may know their sins are forgiven and that there is One Who is with them always, even unto the end of the world.

III

The minister is not likely to adjust himself to the changing environment occasioned by the rise of labor to power unless he asks and answers, "What is in the worker's heart?" The contemporary worker refuses to think of himself as the object of another man's benevolence. He is essential to the economic process and makes a creative contribution that justifies remuneration. He has something to give. He works with others who have something to give. The process involves coöperation and mutual respect. With full allowance for soldiering upon the job and such socially abhorrent practices as featherbedding and all similar activities, the worker is a man who has pride in his work, an individual who knows he is engaged in socially necessary labor. Labor is his life. He looks down upon the parasite and insists that all men shall put in more than they take out. There is a deepening sense of the solidarity of labor. Men refuse to think of themselves as commodities or as machines. They reject the concept that man is a tool to be used by others. The necessities of modern technology have divorced the worker from the ownership of tools. A carpenter or a mechanic may own a few tools of his own but most labor today is applied to great machines that are owned by someone else. Since a worker's life is dependent upon his employment, the term "full employment" carries with it great appeal. The worker knows that the production of wealth involves real labor applied to real material by real machines. The American worker finds little appeal in the utopian nonsense to the effect that all we need to do is draw plans, build our dream cities and live in leisure. It is hard work that lifts the standards of life. What he is interested in is that the productive machine and productive labor may be so related and so directed that production itself shall lift standards because equitably distributed.

The changing environment calls likewise for a full understanding of the underlying philosophy of the trade-union movement. The term itself is a misnomer since the labor movement today is less a matter of organization upon the basis of trade than upon the basis of industry. He must likewise understand Socialism. Men who glibly state that Socialism is Communism ten years earlier are individuals who reveal abysmal ignorance of the subject under discussion. Men discuss Communism who have never read Marx or Lenin or Stalin. Recently the Council of Bishops of the Methodist Church, charged as it is with the temporal and spiritual administration of a world-wide Church, spent a week in study sessions under the leadership of the ablest minds in the United States. The purpose was to seek a full understanding of the Communist challenge to the Christian faith. The Bishops knew that they could not plan for the future of Methodist work in China without full knowledge concerning the thinking of those who rule China today. The program follows:

ARNOLD WOLFERS	"Communism and Nationalism in Soviet Foreign Policy"
SIDNEY HOOK	"The Theory and Strategy of International Communism"
SHERWOOD EDDY	"The Meaning and Menace of Marxian Communism"
LOUIS FISCHER	"The Challenge of Marxist Materialism"
JOHN C. BENNETT	"The Communist Challenge and Christian Strategy"
PAUL B. ANDERSON	"The Development of Communist Approach to Religion and to Contemporary Churches"
MATTHEW SPINKA	"Communism Confronts Christianity"
REINHOLD NIEBUHR	"Communism as a Christian Heresy"
NORMAN THOMAS	"Marxism, Socialism and Communism"
PITIRIM A. SOROKIN	"The Roots and Ways of Resolution of the Russian-American Conflict"

MAX LERNER   "The Meaning and Challenge of Communism"

Subsequently the program was criticized because no Communist had addressed the Bishops. It was argued that no one would think of studying Christianity without having Christians present the Christian faith. The Bishops, however, were aware of the fact that intellectual honesty and Communist tactics are mutually irreconcilable. They preferred a scientific evaluation of Communism by competent scholars to whom truth takes precedence over party interest.

The theological training of the minister which acquaints him with comparative religion is inadequate unless it likewise equips him with a full understanding of the philosophy of Communism, its theory of social development, its economics, its tactics, its concept of dictatorship, and of course the testimony of those who have lived under its rule.

It is of first importance to discover methods by which Christianity may permeate the new world of labor and win the movement for Christ. There are those who insist that the Church is out of its field when it seeks to enter the new environment. The late Archbishop of Canterbury, William Temple, insisted that "the Church has both the right and the duty to declare the principles which should govern the ordering of society. It has this right because, in the revelation entrusted to it, it has the knowledge concerning man and his destiny which depends on that revelation and which illuminates all questions of human conduct. Of course, it is universally recognized that the Church should lay down principles for the conduct of individuals. What lately is being disputed is the right of the Church also to lay down principles for the action of corporate groups, such as trade unions, employers' federations, or national states, or to undertake in any way the direct ordering of men's corporate life. This distinction between individuals and the various groupings in which the lives of individuals are conducted is quite untenable. The whole life of man is conducted in societies. Those societies will, in structure and in function, express the character of those who compose the society and the aims which they have set for themselves. And these, having been expressed in the structure of society, will be reproduced through a process of constant unconscious suggestion in every new generation. The understanding which the Church has concerning the nature of the destiny of man gives it the qualification for declaring what kind of structure in society is wholesome for man and what is unwholesome."

Mr. Frank Gannett, in a pamphlet entitled, "The American Constitution and Its Significance in These Critical Times," declares, "Of the 40,000,000,000 people who have lived on this planet since the birth of Christ, probably not more than three per cent have lived under a government guaranteeing them personal rights, and where they might call their souls their own; where they were something more than herded cattle to be ordered about by someone in power. And a large share of the tiny three per cent who have had any real liberty are those who have lived in this country under our Constitution, since its adoption in 1789." That is a highly significant observation. The overwhelming majority of human beings in the world today have never experienced freedom. This is one of the reasons why the promise of bread is more persuasive than is the pledge of liberty. The people are hungry. They have never known the freedom that is ours. Liberty is thus less an immediate need than is food. This is an important fact in the new environment. Wendell Willkie talked of one world. Others insist there are two worlds. Whatever may be the fact, certain it is that activities in one section of the world have repercussions in all sections. Decision in Washington upon the Marshall Plan determines the course of history in Europe. Refusal to implement President Truman's Point Four and

[44]

thereby share our technical knowledge and invest our capital to the end that living standards may be raised in other parts of the world may give the Communists the very opportunity they covet. Millions of people are beguiled by Communist pledges, in the absence of constructive measures sponsored by free lands. The Christian minister proclaims a world Gospel in the name of a world Saviour, dedicates himself, and, in response to the great Commission, goes "into all the world to teach the nations." His teaching must be backed by the practices of free peoples who stand ready to implement Christian principles with the same courage and sacrifice that the Communist manifests in implementing the Communist ideology. We are our brothers' keeper. Decisions in the United States that reduce import demand in the matter of wool may disrupt the economy of Australia. The passage of a Smoot-Hawley tariff bill may be the Samsonlike pushing out of the stone that brings the financial edifice down upon our heads. The world is one.

Dr. Raymond W. Miller, consultant to the Food and Agricultural Organization of the United Nations, has pointed out that, "Tomorrow, there will be 55,000 more persons for breakfast than there were in the world this morning, the day after tomorrow, 55,000 more, and so on daily—20 to 25 million more people annually. But we are not producing 55,000 more cups of milk a day for the new children, nor 55,000 more loaves of bread, nor 55,000 more bowls of rice. Altogether too many of the world's 2.4 billion population go to bed hungry every night, even in times of normal food production."

The motto of the Food and Agricultural Organization *"Fiat Panis"*—"Let there be bread"—must take its place beside the command at the hour of creation, "Let there be light."

Into the new world must come law and order. But there can be no law and order unless there be light and bread.

Walter Reuther was right when he said, "The issue in

China will not be settled on the battlefields. It will be settled in the rice fields."

IV

To the new environment, the minister must bring a new spirit, a new method, a new objective. Neither economic problems nor international problems can be solved permanently by the methods of war. The industrial history of the United States is a record of conflict. At first, the right of men to organize and to bargain collectively through representatives of their own choosing was denied. There was the attempt to crush out the organization of labor. The work life became a battleground. In conflict, the leaders that emerge are leaders who know how to fight. Had men been driven by the spirit of Jesus, they would have realized that problems are not solved when two-fisted managers square off with two-fisted labor leaders, or similar groups engage in a battle royal while the public pays the price. This was blindness that seems inexcusable today.

Forty years ago, the churches spoke out and said that they stood for "equal rights and complete justice for all men in all stations of life." They called for "the right of employers and employees alike to organize and to bargain collectively through representatives of their own choosing." A political leader recently accused churchmen of being "fuzzy minded" when they deal with economic problems. He might well look back to the recommendations made a generation ago, recommendations that in the last political campaign had become the planks of the parties, and ask where fuzzy mindedness really lies. It results from the refusal to take Jesus of Nazareth seriously. Recently, the economic life of the United States was brought almost to a standstill because of a strike in coal. The problem of coal cannot be solved by the massing of force upon the part of labor nor the similar massing of power upon the part of management. The issues there call for the trained economist, the able executive, for individuals pledged to the ethical ideals of religion. The American coal-miner produces more coal per man than any other miner in the world. This is due to extraordinary advances in equipment and to careful management. It is due, likewise, to the efficiency of the man himself. There may be 100,000 too many men attempting to earn their living in coal today. Are 100,000 men to be thrown upon the labor market? What can a man who has mined coal for thirty years do? These are issues that have to be thought out, rather than fought out. Similarly, in world affairs, the insanity of destroying the wealth of the centuries, of demolishing the productive plants of the world, of killing the flower of our youth, is forcing mankind to recognize that war is the way of madness. Men who contemplate a Third World War and, as an aside, say, "Let's get it over," are men who do not understand that it is blood-soaked soil in which the seeds of communism take root. Millions of men and women and little children who come up from underground shelters with hate in their hearts, hungry and haggard, will follow the demagogue.

Creative minds must give themselves to creative enterprise. It is a time to be *for* something, rather than *against* something. There is much that man must be against. He must be aware of the menace to his freedom that lies in all totalitarian proposals, but the lesson of the last war is clear: defense does not bring victory. It is attack, the forward march, the vision of a better day, instruction, creativity that capture the minds of men who would build rather than destroy. It is into such an environment that the minister comes.

Nicolas Berdyaev, in a lecture delivered in May, 1931, at the congress of the leaders of the Christian World Federation, said:

For Marx, the highest value was not man, but social collectivity. Man is eliminated by the class and a new myth is created, the messianism of the proletariat. Marx is one of the results of humanism. For Nietzsche, the highest value is not man, but superman, the master race; man must be overcome. Nietzsche is the other result of humanism. Thus we behold the renunciation of the value of man, the last value which has survived from Christianity. We observe this, for instance, in such social phenomena as racism, fascism, communism, national idolatry, and international idolatry. We are entering an era of civilization which rejects the value of man. The supreme value of God had been previously rejected. This is the essence of the crisis of our time.

The processes of technicization, the processes of the absorption of the person by society and of collectivization, are all linked to this crisis. All the heresies which arose throughout the history of Christianity, all the negations of the fullness and wholeness of truth, raised serious and significant issues which have not been solved and must be solved by Christianity from within. But the heresies born from our civilization are completely different from the heresies of the first centuries of Christianity; they are not theological heresies, but heresies of life itself. They bear witness to the fact that there are urgent questions which must be answered by Christianity from within. The problems of technology, of the just organization of social life, problems of collectivization in their relation to the eternal value of the human person, have not been solved from within Christianity, in the light of Christian theocratic truth. Man's creative activity in the world has not been consecrated. The crisis taking place in our time is a reminder to Christianity concerning unsolved problems; therefore this crisis is not only a judgment on the godless world, but also a judgment on Christianity.

Humanity has rejected God, but so doing, it has cast doubt not on the dignity of God but on the dignity of man, who cannot maintain himself without God. For humanity, God is precisely that highest idea—that reality which builds man. The reverse aspect of this fact is that man is God's highest idea. Only Christianity solves the problem of man's relations with God; only in Christ the image of man is saved, only in the Christian spirit can a society and a culture be created which do not destroy man. But truth must be realized in life.

THREE

Religious Liberty and the Changing World

THE TOTALITARIAN, WHETHER OF LEFT OR RIGHT, INSISTS
that the State has the right to determine the philosophy
to which every individual who lives within the State must
give assent. George Orwell in "1984" describes the extension
of this shackling and terrifying control until at last the words
expressive of freedom are eliminated from the vocabulary of
the nation and no one is able so much as to phrase the concept of liberty. The words are cut out of dictionaries, removed
from the educational process, and any use of such terms punished so severely that after a time people are deprived of liberty
and the very words necessary to express it.

The Nazi mobilized every impact upon the rising mind—
school, press, church, radio, until at last children and adults
did think in terms of the pre-determined philosophy. It is
true that within Communist and Fascist states guarantees of
religious liberty are written into the Constitution. Such guarantees are meaningless. They are so circumscribed as to make
impossible the application of religion to the social life. Even
where the right to worship is maintained, those who worship

are so controlled in all of their activities and their access to truth so limited that freedom dies. The Church becomes a creature of the State. It is for this, among other reasons, that the doctrine of the separation of Church and State takes on new significance and religious liberty becomes a matter of fundamental importance.

What do we mean by religious liberty? Religious freedom is of course a part of the larger question of liberty itself. Freedom is indivisible.

In May of 1945, at the close of a journey that had taken me through the European and the Mediterranean Theaters of Operation, I boarded a plane at Casablanca. There were ten or fifteen aviators aboard, young men of the Army Air Corps who had been prisoners of the Japanese. One of them, representative of America at its best, told me he had gone down over Burma and had known it meant capture.

"I resolved," he said, "that there were two of my possessions the Japs would never get. I was determined to keep my wedding ring and a little locket my wife had given me. It had her picture in it. Before they lined us up, I put my ring in my shoe, and held my locket so I could 'palm' it. The Japanese officer noted the white circle around my finger where the skin had been protected from the sun by my ring. He pointed to my finger, and said, 'Where is your ring?' I had to give it to him, but I did manage to keep the locket."

The young pilot took the locket out of his pocket and said: "Would you like to see it, Sir?"

"That's my wife," he continued proudly, as he handed it to me.

We talked for a time about his prison experiences, the joy of returning home, the meaning of life, and the future. Finally he said—and there was nothing profane or irreverent in his quiet but intense statement—"God, it is good to be free again."

Men who have lost their freedom become acutely aware of its worth.

Liberty is one of the most treasured words of true Americans. It has found its way into our mint, and when the coins are struck, *liberty* stands out in bold relief. In Philadelphia a broken bell bears the inscription: "Proclaim liberty throughout all the land unto all the inhabitants thereof." Boston has its Faneuil Hall forever associated with the precious words "cradle" and "liberty." Across the Common is the church in which "America" was first sung, "Sweet land of liberty—Land of the noble free—Let freedom ring."

I

What do we mean by religious liberty? The best answer to this question is found in a volume entitled "Religious Liberty: An Inquiry." The Federal Council of the Churches of Christ in America and the Foreign Missions Conference of North America set up a joint committee to consider the whole question of religious liberty. After two years of corporate investigation upon the part of the joint committee, Dr. M. Searle Bates, former Rhodes Scholar and Professor of History of Nanking University, was invited to prepare the basic study. His report was subjected to the most critical consideration, and, after revision, was finally adopted. Kenneth Scott Latourette, the famous historian of Yale University, declares, "There is no other study in this field which so combines comprehensiveness, scholarly competence, objectivity, and penetrating insight." Dr. John A. Mackay, President of the International Missionary Council, was the chairman of the joint committee. In the foreword he wrote:

A new problem has been created for statesmen and churchmen and the mass of common people. Recent events reveal that over large areas of the globe and among powerful human groups a profound change has taken place in thought and attitude with respect to religious freedom. In some instances, freedom of religious expression has totally disappeared. The trend that marked the era of political liberalism, when religious freedom was regarded as an inalienable right possessed by all men, has come to a sudden and dramatic end in large and representative areas of the world. Outside those parts of the world where democracy continues to be taken seriously, no individual can claim religious freedom as an inalienable right. The public implications of his personal faith are determined for him in the name, and in accordance with the interest of some particular group—religious or political—which claims the right and has the power to control his destiny.

The Federal Council of Churches of Christ in America defines religious liberty as follows:

We recognize the dignity of the human person as the image of God. We therefore urge that the civic rights which derive from that dignity be set forth in the agreements into which our country may enter, looking toward the promotion of World Order, and be vindicated in treaty arrangements and in the functions and responsibilities assigned to international organizations. States should assure their citizens freedom from compulsions and discrimination in matters of religion. This and other rights which inhere in man's dignity must be adequately guarded; for when they are impaired, all liberty is jeopardized. More specifically, we urge that:

The right of individuals everywhere to religious liberty shall be recognized and, subject only to the maintenance of public order and security, shall be guaranteed against legal provisions and administrative acts which would impose political, economic or social disabilities on grounds of religion.

Religious liberty shall be interpreted to include freedom of worship according to conscience and to bring up children in the faith of their parents; freedom for the individual to change his religion; freedom to preach, educate, publish, and carry on missionary activities; and freedom to organize with others, and to acquire and hold property for these purposes.

To safeguard public order and to promote the well-being of

the community, both the State, in providing religious liberty, and the people, in exercising the rights thus recognized, must fulfill reciprocal obligations. The State must guard all groups, both minority and majority, against legal disabilities on account of religious beliefs; the people must exercise their rights with a sense of responsibility, and with charitable consideration for the rights of others.

The World Council of Churches at Amsterdam adopted a Declaration on Religious Liberty and in formal resolution urged the application of its provisions through domestic and international action. The Declaration is of such fundamental importance that it is quoted in its entirety.

An essential element in a good international order is freedom of religion. This is an implication of the Christian faith and of the world-wide nature of Christianity. Christians, therefore, view the question of religious freedom as an international problem. They are concerned that religious freedom be everywhere secured. In pleading for this freedom, they do not ask for any privilege to be granted to Christians that is denied to others. While the liberty with which Christ has set men free can neither be given nor destroyed by any government, Christians, because of that inner freedom, are both jealous for its outward expression and solicitous that all men should have freedom in religious life. The nature and destiny of man by virtue of his creation, redemption and calling, and man's activities in family, state and culture establish limits beyond which the government cannot with impunity go. The rights which Christian discipleship demands are such as are good for all men, and no nation has ever suffered by reason of granting such liberties. Accordingly:

The rights of religious freedom herein declared shall be recognized and observed for all persons without distinction as to race, colour, sex, language or religion, and without imposition of disabilities by virtue of legal provisions or administrative acts.

1. Every person has the right to determine his own faith and creed.

The right to determine faith and creed involves both the process whereby a person adheres to a belief and the process whereby he changes his belief. It includes the right to receive instruction and education.

This right becomes meaningful when man has the opportunity of access to information. Religious, social and political institutions have the obligation to permit the mature individual to relate himself to sources of information in such a way as to allow personal religious decisions and belief.

The right to determine one's belief is limited by the right of parents to decide sources of information to which their children shall have access.

In the process of reaching decisions, everyone ought to take into account his higher self-interests and the implications of his beliefs for the wellbeing of his fellow men.

2. Every person has the right to express his religious beliefs in worship, teaching and practice, and to proclaim the implications of his beliefs for relationships in a social or political community.

The right of religious expression includes freedom of worship, both public and private; freedom to place information at the disposal of others by processes of teaching, preaching and persuasion; and freedom to pursue such activities as are dictated by conscience. It also includes freedom to express implications of belief for society and its government.

This right requires freedom from arbitrary limitation of religious expression in all means of communication, including speech, press, radio, motion pictures and art. Social and political institutions should grant immunity from discrimination and from legal disability on grounds of expressed religious conviction, at least to the point where recognized community interests are adversely affected.

Freedom of religious expression is limited by the rights of parents to determine the religious point of view to which their children shall be exposed. It is further subject to such limitations, prescribed by law, as are necessary to protect order and welfare, morals and the rights and freedoms of others. Each person must recognize the right of others to express their beliefs and must have respect for authority at all times, even when his conscience forces him to take issue with the people who are in authority or with the position they advocate.

3. Every person has the right to associate with others and to organize with them for religious purposes.

This right includes freedom to form religious organizations, to seek membership in religious organizations, and to sever relationship with religious organizations.

It requires that the rights of association and organization guaranteed by a community to its members include the right of forming associations for religious purposes.

It is subject to the same limits imposed on all associations by non-discriminatory laws.

4. Every religious organization, formed or maintained by action in accordance with the rights of individual persons, has the right to determine its policies and practices for the accomplishment of its chosen purposes.

The rights which are claimed for the individual in his exercise of religious liberty become the rights of the religious organization, including the right to determine its faith and creed; to engage in religious worship, both public and private; to teach, educate, preach and persuade; to express implications of belief for society and government. To these will be added certain corporate rights which derive from the rights of individual persons, such as the right; to determine the form of organization, its government and conditions of membership; to select and train its own officers, leaders and workers; to publish and circulate religious literature; to carry on service and missionary activities at home and abroad; to hold property and to collect funds; to co-operate and to unite with other religious bodies at home and in other lands, including freedom to invite or to send personnel beyond national frontiers and to give or to receive financial assistance; to use such facilities, open to all citizens or associations, as will make possible the accomplishment of religious ends.

In order that these rights may be realized in social experience, the state must grant to religious organizations and their members the same rights which it grants to other organizations, including the right of self-government, of public meeting, of speech, of press and publication, of holding property, of collecting funds, of travel, of ingress and egress, and generally of administering their own affairs.

The community has the right to require obedience to non-discriminatory laws passed in the interest of public order and well-being. In the exercise of its rights, a religious organization must respect the rights of other religious organizations and must safeguard the corporate and individual rights of the entire community.

On December 10, 1948, the General Assembly of the United Nations adopted a Universal Declaration of Human Rights. Article XVIII reads:

"Everyone has the right to freedom of thought, conscience and religion; this right includes freedom to change his religion or belief, and freedom, either alone or in community with others, and in public or private, to manifest his religion or belief in teaching, practice, worship and observance."

Christians are properly proud of the decisive contributions made by the Federal Council of the Churches of Christ in America and of the World Council of Churches through its Commission of the Churches on International Affairs to this Declaration. Several years of painstaking research, negotiation, and brotherly insistence lie back of that Article.

Religious liberty and, for that matter, all civil liberties are abrogated within the totalitarian state for the very simple reason that totalitarianism and civil liberty are mutually exclusive. Rewinning such liberties for Church and citizen will involve years of struggle, fearless witness upon the part of the individual, development of a world public opinion that repudiates repression, and within areas that are free, the dedication of free men to the practice of the moral law in society. Immediate action can be taken within the Church itself. All doctrines and practices within the control of the Church that are in themselves denials of the concept of religious liberty must be re-examined and proper steps taken for their revision or rejection.

The history of the Roman Catholic church and of the Protestant churches is marred by intolerance, denials of religious liberty and at times outright persecution. American soldiers died upon foreign soil not alone to destroy the totalitarian threat to freedom but also to establish freedom everywhere. One of the four freedoms is Freedom of Religion. The Church ought to be the first and strongest defender of religious liberty.

I am quite certain that I speak the mind of American Protestantism when I say that it is the desire of every thoughtful and devoted Protestant to secure for every Roman Catholic and for the Roman Catholic church the same religious liberty that Protestants demand for themselves and their churches. Insofar as intolerance of any kind has been a part of Protestant practice in the past or manifests itself anywhere in the present, repentance and works meet for repentance are required.

Monsignor Fulton J. Sheen, in a recent radio sermon, suggested that pride must give way to humility before the redemptive work of the Holy Spirit can be consummated in the heart of a sinner. That is true and it is equally true of an institution. It applies to the Protestant churches, the Roman Catholic church and the Jewish synagogues.

Too often, dynamic faith is institutionalized for purposes of propagation. There is always danger that men of lesser stature than the founders may come to regard the institution as of more significance than the faith. Their major energy is spent in keeping the institution going rather than in using the institution as a means to permeate society with the spirit of Jesus and to transform the human soul. Knowing Protestantism as I do, I know the danger that lies in regarding the Church as an end in itself rather than as a means to do the will of the Lord. I am quite certain, nevertheless, that there is a deep and determined resolve throughout the Protestant churches of the United States to maintain and to extend religious liberty until at last every man shall possess the precious privilege of worshipping God according to the dictates of his own conscience.

II

The statements of the Roman Catholic church upon the subject of religious liberty and the practices in countries in which the Roman Catholic church is the dominant religious community give Protestants grave concern. There are many who see a fundamental trend toward clericalism in the United States. It is their belief that clericalism curses those who practice it and develops reactions that divide the religious and political life of the community. Dr. John A. Mackay, President of Princeton Theological Seminary, defines clericalism as, "The pursuit of power, especially political power, by a religious hierarchy, carried on by secular methods, and for purposes of social domination."

Pope Leo XIII in *Immortale Dei* declared, "It is not lawful for the State . . . to hold in equal favor different kinds of religion." In the famous Syllabus of Errors, issued in 1864, the proposition, "The Church ought to be separated from the State, and the State from the Church" is specifically condemned. The proposition, "Every man is free to embrace and profess the religion he shall believe true, guided by the light of reason" is likewise condemned and repudiated. In the authoritative volume, written and edited for the Department of Social Action of the National Catholic Welfare Conference by Professor John A. Ryan, D.D., and Morehouse F.X. Millar, a Jesuit father, bearing the imprimatur of Archbishop Hayes, and passing through several editions, it is declared: "The fact that the individual may in good faith think that his false religion is true gives him no more right to propagate it than the sincerity of the alien anarchist entitles him to advocate his abominable political theories in the United States."

One of the clearest and frankest statements of Roman Catholic teaching is found in a pamphlet entitled "Freedom of Worship, the Catholic Position," written by Francis J. Connell, C.SS.R., S.T.D., published by the Paulist Press and carrying the imprimatur of Cardinal Spellman. Father Connell says:

Catholics believe that the Catholic Church is the only organization authorized by God to teach religious truth and to conduct public religious worship. Consequently, they hold that any creed which differs from that of the Catholic Church is erroneous, and that any religious organization which is separated from the Catholic Church lacks the approval and the authorization of God. The very existence of any other church is opposed to the command of Christ that all men should join His one Church.

From this it follows that, as far as God's law is concerned, no one has a real right to accept any religion save the Catholic religion, or to be a member of any church save the Catholic Church, or to practice any form of divine worship save that commanded or sanctioned by the Catholic Church. At first sight, this claim may seem arrogant. It certainly presents a striking contrast to the statement we hear so frequently today, that everyone has a perfect, inalienable right to practice any form of religion he wishes. But a little thought will show that the Catholic position is perfectly reasonable. Any person who believes in a personal God to whom all creatures are subject must admit that He is entitled to command all men to accept and to practice one particular form of religion. Now, Catholics hold that God has actually done this—that He has imposed on all men the obligation to accept and to practice Catholicism, the religion founded by the divine Redeemer of the world. Logically then, Catholics hold that no one has a genuine right, as far as God's law is concerned, to profess any religion except the Catholic religion. Certainly, no creature has a genuine right to disobey the command of God.

. . . It was in accord with this principle that Pope Pius IX, in his Syllabus of 1864, condemned the proposition: "Every man is free to embrace and profess that religion which guided by the light of reason, he judged true. . . . The mere fact that a person sincerely believes a religion to be true gives him no genuine right to accept that religion in opposition to God's command that all must embrace the one true religion. Neither does it necessarily oblige others to allow him the unrestricted practice of his religious beliefs. . . ."

The second Catholic principle, pertinent to freedom of worship can be called, by contrast to the first, the principle of personal tolerance. It is simply an application of Christ's commandment: "Thou shalt love thy neighbor as thyself." Catholics consider themselves bound to love all human beings without exception— not for merely natural or humanitarian reasons, but because every human being possesses a spiritual, immortal soul, made to the image and likeness of God, destined to be the temple of God in this life and to be a citizen of His eternal kingdom in the life to come. This supernatural love must embrace not only Catholics, but also Protestants, Jews, Mohammedans, Buddhists, pagans, atheists—in a word, all men without exception, irrespective of their religious belief or unbelief. It must be a generous, self-sacrificing love; it must include the willingness to help those who are in need, whatever may be their religious persuasions.

Because of this duty of supernatural love toward all, Catholics must presume that those who differ from them in religion are sincere, unless the opposite is manifest. While Catholics are always glad to point out to others the reasonable ground for the acceptance of Catholicity, they would do wrong if they tried to induce a non-Catholic to enter the Catholic Church against the sincere conviction of his own conscience. For no one possessing the use of reason may affiliate himself with the Catholic Church unless he is intellectually persuaded of the truth of Catholicity. Now it is certainly possible for a non-Catholic in all sincerity to be convinced that his own religion is true. According to Catholic principles, such a person is obliged in conscience to continue the practice of his religion, and Catholics respect his sincerity, even though they are convinced he has not a genuine right to profess a religion differing from that which the Son of God commanded all men to accept. Catholics may not persecute non-Catholics because of their sincere religious convictions. However, as was pointed out above, this does not necessarily imply that unrestricted freedom must be granted by Catholics to the religious activities of non-Catholics.

If the country is distinctively Catholic—that is, if the population is almost entirely Catholic, and the national life and institutions are permeated with the spirit of Catholicity—the civil rulers can consider themselves justified in restricting or preventing denominational activities hostile to the Catholic religion. This does not mean that they may punish or persecute those who do not accept the Catholic faith. But they are justified in repressing written or spoken attacks on Catholicism, the use of the press or the mails to weaken the allegiance of Catholics toward their Church, and similar anti-Catholic efforts.

Nevertheless, even in a predominantly Catholic country, circumstances may render it more advisable for the government to grant non-Catholics the same measures of freedom of worship as is enjoyed by Catholics. Such a course is justifiable when it is foreseen that a policy of complete toleration will procure greater good than will repressive measures against anti-Catholic activities.

In a country like the United States, where the religious affiliations of the citizens are so numerous and so diverse, and where no single denomination is predominant, complete equality for all religions is undoubtedly the most commendable policy. From what has been said above, and from the example of Catholic Ireland, it is very evident that only one who is ignorant of Catholic teaching can assert that if Catholics ever gained the balance of political power in the United States they would be obliged by their principles to impose restrictions on their non-Catholic fellow-citizens. The Catholics of America are just as anxious as their Protestant and Jewish neighbors to maintain and to promote civil equality for all religions throughout our land.

In Spain, Dr. Searle M. Bates records:

According to reports of the year 1944, it seems that twenty out of two hundred Protestant churches are now open. Some pastors have been driven out of the country, and others work under persecution, covert or naked. All Protestant schools were closed. In the larger cities, members are able to get along, but in smaller communities recognized Protestants were commonly refused employment, sale of goods, and government relief. No Spaniard can secure a certificate for leaving school or can he enter civil service, until he has official evidence of instruction in the Roman Catholic religion. Every officer and soldier must attend mass. In the rural districts, copies of the Bible have been taken, even from individuals. Despite earlier permission from the present regime to print and to circulate, since 1940 the Bible Society has been ordered by the Under Secretary for Press and Propaganda, acting under instructions from the Minister of the Interior, to stop circulation of the Scriptures. Police, under the same order, confiscated the 100,-000 pieces of bound items kept in Madrid. Bibles are stopped at the frontier. (In the last normal year, steady increase in sales had reached 211,000 copies). In Spain, the Church, which suffered so grievously and fought so fiercely under the banner of freedom, has shown again that it desired not religious liberty but Roman Catholic monopoly.[1]

In Peru, the Pastoral Letter issued by the Archbishops and Bishops as late as December 18, 1943, declared:

We are in duty bound to raise today a warning voice against a grave and widespread danger which seriously threatens the purity and unity of our religious faith. The fold has already been daringly attacked, and the wolf would continue with immunity to spoil the flock and enjoy at the same time the protection of the law and the good will of the authorities. . . . Many years ago now, Protestantism commenced to filter through into this nation. . . . The first groups, however, worked very much behind the scenes, since the Fourth Article of our Constitution declared the Apostolic Roman Catholic faith to be the state religion to the exclusion of all other forms of worship. The Protestant sects, however, in combination with anti-Catholic societies, refused to rest until they had succeeded by specious pretexts in inducing our Legislative Chambers first to mutilate and later repeal this Article which constituted

[1] "Religious Liberty: An Inquiry," page 20.

a sacred bulwark of our religious belief and a powerful restraint against sectarian audacity. . . . Scarcely was this protecting wall broken down and liberty of worship granted than the unrestrained violence of the sects overflowed in campaigns to propagate their doctrines; and, as though they now owned the country, they abused the hospitality so liberally extended to them and thought themselves quite within their rights in setting to work to demolish the secular edifice of our Catholicism by applying to it the incendiary torch of their heretical blasphemy. . . . We see them posing as teachers of religion, belching forth upon the ignorant populace from their soap boxes in streets, plazas and parks, the whole content of their falsehood, pitifully disfiguring the very foundations of dogma and ethics, disguising the Word of God, deliberately falsifying historical truth. . . . To insure the success of their work, they carefully choose outlying suburbs and places where the presence of priests, missionaries, or energetic Catholics does not interfere with the de-Christianization of the humble poor. . . . How is it they prefer our territory for the scene of their evangelical aggression and forget the 75,000,000 of atheists which figure in the latest census in the United States?

Then follows an attempt to introduce the factor of patriotism. The Pastoral Letter continues:

Whoever attempts to violate our spiritual unity, attacks, therefore, our nationality. . . . Outstanding writers attribute to the Protestant campaign of propaganda purposes that go further than a mere propagation of sects, the agents of which are these Protestants so long prepared and well paid. . . . It is urgent, therefore, that we undermine and counteract the Protestant campaign, which is a crusade of error and lies, opposing it with a sound and vigorous Crusade of Prayer and Apostleship. . . . This should be organized, as we have noted, on a plan of resistance and action against Protestantism with the collaboration of all the vital forces of Catholicism.

In Mexico, a Pastoral Letter of similar spirit was followed by violence in which Protestant churches were destroyed and

Protestant preachers attacked and brutally beaten. Subsequently, the violence reached such a pitch that several were killed.

A letter dated September 21, 1949, written in Cochabamba, Bolivia, by a distinguished Protestant missionary, records:

We have been proud of our Protestant people. For several weeks before the revolution, the Protestants had been the objective of an organized attack by the Roman hierarchy, which resulted in the deaths of nine Protestants in a town near here (two of them dear friends of ours), and in two vicious attacks fortunately not fatal, on Protestants in Cochabamba. The first of these were organized by the nuns who administer the public hospital here, and the second by the priest of the hospital chapel. The reaction of our people is typically illustrated by one of our fine young Bolivians who was scheduled to go to Buenos Aires next year for his theological studies. I told him about the rather horrible deaths of our brothers in the Faith with some misgivings. After a long silence, he said: "Now I see more clearly than ever that God calls me to the Ministry. If pastors are to be killed, we must have many, many more of them so as not to be overcome."

The memorial service here, in which all the protestants in Cochabamba co-operated, was a strange and beautiful meeting. One after another of those present, from humble Indians to educated gentlemen, testified as to the lives of service of the martyrs. There was at no point any bitterness toward our persecutors, but rather a constant prayer to God to give us strength so that we might overcome hate with love, and withstand whatever might be in store for us.

III

Much of this grows out of the past. It is the present that we confront. Religious liberty in the changing world becomes increasingly the concern of all. The Roman Catholic church suffers severely under the ruthless attack of Communism. Distinguished prelates have been tortured and imprisoned.

Both Cardinal Mindszenty of the Roman Catholic church and Bishop Ordass of the Lutheran church were imprisoned in Hungary. Protestant pastors have suffered a similar fate in Bulgaria. They are caught between the jaws of the Communist vise. Upon one side is the resolve to impose an ideology; upon the other, is the determination to deny religious, or, for that matter, any liberty that in any way endangers the regime. With each turn, the jaws move closer together. Those caught within them are destroyed. It is to the interest of all religious groups everywhere to resist these denials of liberty; but those who come into court upon this issue must come with clean hands, Protestant, Jew and Roman Catholic alike.

It is unfortunately true that the Roman Catholic hierarchy holds to a principle that is a denial of religious liberty. Where opposition to the principle is strong, it practices tolerance as a temporary expedient. The latter must be judged by the former. A doctrine of expediency has no place in the realm of religious liberty. Either we believe in religious liberty or we do not.

Churches that hold to any principles that deny religious liberty must repudiate them. Liberty itself is in jeopardy. There is a very simple rule that can govern in all matters of religious freedom. It comes from the highest Authority, "Do unto others as ye would be done by." Professor A. Victor Murray, President of Cheshunt College, at the jubilee of the Free Church Council meeting in London, pointed out "Rome nowadays is represented by a sectarian type of organization. It believes itself to be the perfect society, judge in its own cause, omnicompetent and self-sufficient. Anything that furthers its interests, political or social, as well as religious, is considered to be according to the will of God. Mussolini's expedition to Abyssinia furthered the interests of Romanism, and was blessed by the Pope. Franco's rebellion in Spain was helped by a large donation from the Archbishop of Seville.

The Vatican has been as busy as the Communists in separating Poles from Poles in Warsaw. It is the irresponsible influence in an internationally organized society with its headquarters in a foreign country—in this way exactly parallel to Communism—that makes the free church Protestant evangelical witness against Rome so vitally necessary."

IV

In the American scene, a new emphasis upon the principle of the separation of Church and State is essential.

One of the best and briefest statements of the essentials of this doctrine is found in an address delivered by Charles Clayton Morrison, former editor of *The Christian Century*, when he spoke to the International Convention of the Disciples of Christ. He said:

There are four ways in which the Church may be related to the State. The Church may be above the State, or below the State, or in alliance with the State, or side by side with the State in a free society. First, then, the Church may be above the State. This is the Roman Catholic theory. That Church claims itself to be a supernational State. Second, the Church may be below the State, subordinate to it, serving the State, conforming its teaching to the ideology of the State and sanctifying the actions and authority of the State. This is totalitarianism. Third, the Church may be organically allied with the State, so that the State provides for its support by taxation. This is the theory of the established or state church.

The fourth way in which church and state may be related is the American way. Here church and state exist side by side, but completely separate and independent, in a free society. This arrangement is peculiarly congenial to democracy. The Constitution of the United States forbids any legislation respecting the establishment of religion or any interference with the free exercise thereof.

The American people were determined that their new state

should not be a totalitarian state. True, they did not have the word, "totalitarian," but they very clearly had that idea when they insisted upon a bill of rights. They were determined to keep outside the scope of government the whole cultural domain—the domain of belief, of conscience, of speech, of publication, of scientific research, of assembly, of worship, together with the institutions which embodied these liberties. They drew a circle around government, and proclaimed that the entire area outside that circle was a realm of freedom—free action, free opinion, free inquiry, free discussion, free persuasion, free decision, free education. Religion was specifically named as lying outside the government's jurisdiction. The American state thus became the guarantor of a free pulpit, a free altar and a free church.

The state guarantees this freedom by completely separating its own function as government from the institutional functioning of the church. With religious freedom it will not interfere. It will not establish any religion as the religion of the state. It will not grant special favor or privilege to any religion. Nor will it put any religion under the ban of government. And it will not allow the official processes of government to be meshed or interlocked with the official processes of any church. The theory of our democracy thus completely separates the functions of political government from the functions of organized religion. This is religious liberty.

What then do we mean by separation of church and state? Let us be clear in our use of words. We do not mean separation of religion and the state, nor separation of religion and politics, nor yet separation of the church and politics. We mean separation of church and state—a concept wholly different from any of those just mentioned. The church is the organized institution of religion, just as the state is the organized institution of political life. It is these two institutions which must be kept separate, according to our constitution and our American tradition. But it is a separation which still leaves room for moral and spiritual interaction and responsiveness. In what respect, then, are these institutions to be kept separate? The answer is that they are to be kept separate—completely separate—in their official or institutional functioning. The official functioning of the state must be kept separate from the official functioning of the church. There must be no entanglement of their respective processes by law or by the administration of law.

In this connection, it is well to remember that Federal Judge Leon R. Yankwich says in a recent article, entitled "The Background of the American Bill of Rights," that:

A State which brooks no opposition will enslave its people, whether it does so under the pretense of an economic, racial, social, or cultural ideal. . . . Under the authoritarian State, the individual is only the means or instrument of society's end; whatever rights and values the individual has he has derived from the omnipotent State. The American Bill of Rights recognizes the absolute right of individuals before the State. Indeed, the first ten Amendments are merely confirmatory of existing rights. They do not bestow them.

Judge Yankwich is correct. The rights of the individuals who compose the American community are absolute. They are not conferred.

Dean Luther A. Weigle of Yale University approaches the issue from another point of view, and wisely warns:

The Separation of Church and State is a sound principle, but one that is much misunderstood. It properly means that Church and State are mutually free, and that neither may rightfully control the other. But it does not mean that Church and State, being mutually free, cannot cooperate with one another. And it does not mean that the State acknowledges no God, or that the State is exempt from the moral law wherewith God sets the bounds of justice for nations as well as for individuals. Let us clearly understand, moreover, that the separation of Church and State does not require the separation of civic duty and religious faith. A State degenerates into tyranny if its citizens abandon conscience when they approach the polls and forget God when they are in public office. And no man has true religion who reserves it for home or Sunday or heaven or a catacomb or a "retreat" and fails to use it as a resource for daily living and for public service. The phrase "the separation of Church and State" has been somewhat over-worked in recent years. It stands for only one aspect of the more comprehensive principle of religious freedom. Experience has shown that a high degree of religious freedom can be secured without the separation of Church and State, as in Great Britain, and, on the other hand, that the separation of Church and State does not itself insure the full religious freedom of minority groups, as in Russia. The phrase, moreover, is merely negative. It too easily lends itself to the idea that State and Church are without common interest, that they should have nothing to do with one another, and that the State should be purely secular, without God, above or below the moral law, and, in short, belong to the devil. It too easily lends itself, again, to the idea that the Church has no concern save freedom to worship. The problems of religious freedom, of the relations between State and Church, and of the enmeshing in human life of power, reason and conscience are too vast and intricate to be solved by simply shouting for the separation of Church and State. The truth is that religious freedom is not a special privilege which the State affords to folk of peculiar temper. It is a right which has entered into the very nature of the State. It is one of the basic freedoms in any sound bill of rights. Historically, logically, and in practice, it undergirds and sustains human democracy. It is of the very essence of democracy. Without religious freedom, all other freedoms are in danger.

It is true that the statement of the principle by some would indicate a separation of religion itself from the life of the State. This would be disastrous. The principle itself, however, as defined by Dr. Morrison and as practiced through American history, has proved its worth and is sound. It reaffirms the American doctrine that the State shall not play religious favorites. It gives to all religious groups full opportunity to grow in terms of their ability to win the minds and hearts of men. It is in this freedom and under this practice that mutual respect develops and the national life becomes religiously based.

V

One of the current issues that carries with it the question of American culture itself is that of supporting parochial or private education with public funds. The Roman Catholic hierarchy has sought to reach the public treasury in order to secure public funds for the support of sectarian education.

The Roman Catholic church is opposed to our system of public education. It is true that the Most Rev. John T. Mc-Nicholas, Archbishop of Cincinnati, said, "Let it be said, with all possible emphasis, that the Catholic Church is not opposed to tax-supported schools. On the contrary, she heartily endorses our compulsory system of education in America; she sincerely commends the traditional freedom of American education, and also the generous spirit of America to make adequate provision for education, which generosity will again be manifested to our teachers in the post-war crisis through which we are passing." This quotation appears upon a pamphlet entitled, "No Wall Between God and the Child" circulated by the National Catholic Welfare Conference, Department of Education, during American Education Week, November 9–15, 1947. It should be noted that Archbishop Mc-Nicholas referred to "tax-supported schools" and "a compulsory system of education." The use of these terms makes it possible for the Archbishop to be consistent with authoritative Catholic teaching, since of course he can have a tax-supported parochial system and the compulsory feature can be included in that system. Catholic teaching expressly forbids Roman Catholic children to attend public schools, except under special conditions. Pope Pius XI, in an Encyclical dated January 16, 1930, wrote:

Attendance at non-Catholic, neutral, or mixed schools—schools, that is to say, indifferently open to Catholics and non-Catholics without distinction—is forbidden to Catholic children and can only be tolerated at the discretion of bishops in special circumstances of place and time and under special precautions. Neither is it admissible for Catholics to attend mixed schools—worse still, if obligatory for all—where religious instruction is provided and pupils receive the rest of their teaching from non-Catholic masters, together with non-Catholic children. . . . For a school to be acceptable, it is necessary that the whole teaching and organization of the school—namely, the teachers, the curriculum and the books —is governed by the Christian spirit, under the maternal direction and vigilance of the Church.

We are all familiar with the statement by Father Paul L. Blakely of the Society of Jesus in his pamphlet, "May an American Oppose the Public School?" He wrote:

Our first duty to the public school is not to pay taxes for its maintenance. . . . The first duty of each Catholic father to the public school is to keep his children out of it.

The issue here is not the right of a church to maintain schools to educate its children, if the parents so desire. No one questions that right. Whether it be wise to send our children to parochial schools during childhood is another question. Personally, I prefer the public schools. I am proud of the fact that my Protestant sons and daughter had the privilege of sitting in classrooms with their Roman Catholic and other friends, Jew by Gentile, black by white, foreign-born by native-born, and there learned to live together in mutual respect— not as Protestants, Roman Catholics, Jews, Gentiles, Negroes, and whites, but as Americans, and children of one Father.

But the question of public support for parochial education does raise the issue of the separation of Church and State.

In confronting the issue of Federal aid to education, the distinguished John Courtney Murray tells us, "It would be a great gain, too, if it were agreed to drop the deceptive formula 'separation of Church and State'." But it is precisely that formula which is a statement of basic principle, and we will not drop it. To drain off vast sums for the support of competing sectarian systems of education is, in the long run, to destroy our public system. The attack of the Roman Catholic hierarchy upon this principle has as its ultimate objective the establishment of "ideal conditions." If the hierarchy can breach the wall and secure public support of parochial education, it will have gained a substantial position where it will stand until it is ready for further advance.

On May 24, 1943, the National Catholic Welfare Conference addressed a letter to Senator Elbert D. Thomas during hearings involving Federal aid to education. That letter stated, "The Catholic position is one of opposition to any measures for education that would (a) interfere with local control of the purposes and processes of education and (b) fail to make mandatory the inclusion of Catholic schools in its benefits." It is entirely proper to raise the question of Federal control of education. Many hold that support often means control. If bills can be drawn to avoid this danger, the Roman Catholic church, according to this statement, would still oppose this evident good unless public funds are used to support parochial education. Of course, the hierarchy in Spain does not believe in public support of Protestant education. As a matter of fact, no Spaniard can secure a certificate for leaving school or can enter the civil service unless he has official evidence of instruction in the Roman Catholic religion. The Most Rev. John T. McNicholas, when President General of the National Catholic Education Association, in a pamphlet entitled, "Federal Aid for American Education," wrote, "Marriage implies the right to procreate and to educate children. This right does not come from the State or from any civil or ecclesiastical authorities; it comes from nature and from God." It is interesting that he should include ecclesiastical as well as civil authority in the statement. However, he covers the matter a little later on by saying, referring to parents,

"They must also recognize that the Church in the spiritual order, is divinely commissioned to teach their children the things of God and to prepare them for their eternal destiny."

The Roman Catholic position logically calls upon every parent to determine the education of his children and, if schools satisfactory to the views of the parents are not available, then the parents must associate themselves with other parents and establish schools to their liking and call upon the people to support these schools. Does the hierarchy really mean this? If so, does the hierarchy honestly hold that a Communist parent has the same duty and should be granted the same privileges?

Is the Communist father to determine the education of his child, to build Communist schools and call upon the rest of us to pay the bill? Personally, I do not want public money to be used to support Communist schools, Fascist schools, Roman Catholic schools or Protestant schools. Public money should be used to support public schools. I do not want public support of private education that rears a child in a philosophy of materialism, in Marxian economics, in the Communist theory of social development or in an acceptance of the method of dictatorship, whether temporary or permanent. In a word, I do not wish public support for Communist schools. Nor do I want public support of Fascist schools where Nazi paganism or Mussolini methodologies are taught. Neither do I want public funds used in parochial education where historic fact is sometimes suppressed to glorify the Church and undemocratic papal pronouncements are given undue prominence.

It was my privilege to serve on the President's Commission on Higher Education. The Commission faced this issue, and reached the conclusion "Federal funds for the general support of current educational activities and for general capital outlay purposes should be appropriated for use only in institutions under public control. Sound public policy demands, furthermore, that State and local public educational bodies be able to exercise at all times the right to review and control educational policies in any institution or agency for which public monies are appropriated and expended. Public responsibility for support of education implies public responsibility for the policies which are supported."

If we begin upon this policy of public support for parochial education, where do we stop? Is there to be a Methodist system of education, an Episcopalian, a Baptist? Are all to be supported by public funds? There are more than seven hundred colleges and universities related to the churches, more than five hundred are Protestant. What, too, of the great institutions of learning on private foundations? Anyone acquainted with the problem of budget-balancing in private education or with great needs and opportunities in research and service that remain unmet until private philanthropy makes funds available, knows the demands upon public treasuries would soon be mountain-high. And who decides how much and when? The real value that lies in a private system, side by side with a public system of education, is lost the minute the private system is supported by the public. There are values in experimentation, in different emphases. But does anyone believe for a moment that public support will not involve public regulation at the local level much stricter than the present regulation in terms of standards? Is a Jew to pay taxes for the support of Roman Catholic parochial education when he believes in some quarters the emphasis is of such a nature as to contribute to anti-Semitism? Such matters would sooner or later be in the courts. Is it not the course of wisdom to maintain our right to private education by supporting that education privately?

All of us, Roman Catholic, Protestant and Jew, enjoy freedom in this land. It should not be jeopardized by the demand for public support. There is no state church here. The people who love the Church support it. There is a public school here, and the public supports it. That is as it should be. We want neither clericalism nor anti-clericalism in this land. The attempt to win public support for parochial education is ill conceived, will divide us, and must be defeated.

There is no constitutional prohibition of the study of religion in the public school. The difficulty stems rather from denominational differences and insistences upon a particular emphasis. The place of religion, all religions, in history, sociology, art, music, literature, must be known by educated men and women. To rear youth without knowledge of the place of religion in life is to educate them partially. But Church and Synagogue do more than study religion as a subject; they seek to convert. This is not the function of the school.

The report of the American Council of Education, entitled "The Relation of Religion to Public Education," sums the matter up, as follows:

The exclusion of religion from the public school which so largely prevails today results in its relegation in the minds of youth to a position of relative unimportance. This runs counter, we believe, to the intent of the American school system from the beginning. On the other hand, any educational innovation which would tend to identify public education with a particular body of sectarian beliefs and practices we hold to be not only impractical but improper. . . . Holding to the separation of Church and State in America, we nevertheless deplore what we consider the strange application of this principle in our school systems. We are unable to believe that a school which accepts responsibility for bringing its students into full possession of their cultural heritage can be considered to have performed its task if it leaves them without a knowledge of the role of religion in our history, its relation to other phases of the culture, and the ways in which the religious life of the American community is expressed.

[75]

The leaders of American public education and the teaching staff are in overwhelming majority religious men and women. They are deeply concerned with the spiritual and moral development of the child. The place of religion in the public schools could be worked out democratically without too great difficulty were it not for sectarian strife. Americans must not be induced to attack the public school system by a church that is pursuing its own interests.

When we are confronted with the demand for public support of parochial education, it is proper to ask what is being taught in the schools we are called upon to support. The Catechism used in the schools of Spain says that,

The principal errors condemned by the Church are thirteen.

It lists among them Protestantism, Liberalism, and Free Masonry. In question and answer form, the Catechism states the position of the Church, as follows:

Q. What are the freedoms which Liberalism defends?

A. Freedom of conscience, freedom of worship, and freedom of the press.

Q. What does freedom of the press mean?

A. The right to print and publish without previous censorship all kinds of opinions, however absurd and corrupting they may be.

Q. Must the Government suppress this freedom by means of censorship?

A. Obviously, yes.

Q. Why?

A. Because it must prevent the deception, calumny and corruption of its subjects which harm the general good.

Q. Are there other pernicious freedoms?

A. Yes. Freedom of education, freedom of propaganda, and freedom of assembly.

Q. Why are these freedoms pernicious?

A. Because they serve to teach error, propagate vice, and plot against the Church.

[76]

It may be said, "But, after all, that is Spain. This is America." That is true. It is also true that Roman Catholic policies are determined in Rome, not in the United States. However, the Catechism in the "Manual of Christian Doctrine" used in parochial schools in the United States and which carries the imprimatur of Cardinal Dougherty of Philadelphia, is very similar.

A request to quote from the Catechism was refused on the ground that the Manual of Christian Doctrine was first printed in 1902, even though it was reprinted in 1943. The refusal stated: "The presentation on Church and State relations is not at all adequate for present day conditions particularly in this country." But children in Roman Catholic schools are taught this material, which is in strict accord with the official views of Roman Catholicism on the question of civil liberty. The Catechism specifically rejects separation of church and state, and condemns liberty of conscience and of worship, liberty of speech and press.

The maintenance of religious liberty throughout the world is directly related to the reconciliation of the differences that exist in the United States of America today. This nation stands as a bulwark against the denials of liberty, political, economic, and religious, inherent in totalitarianism. There ought to be some way in the interest of unity to resolve the present conflict between Roman Catholic and Protestant. Millions of Roman Catholic Americans, reared in the tradition of American freedom, are restive under the exercise by the hierarchy of mediaeval notions of power.

One of the chief barriers to reconciliation lies in the fact that the Roman Catholic church insists upon being both a state and a church. The Pope is not only the head of a church but also the head of a state. He speaks as the head of a world church, with spiritual interests, and also speaks as the head of a state with political and financial interests. Unfortunately, this set-up means that the Roman Catholic church seeks to advance its political interests as a state and the Roman Catholic political parties in European nations follow the Vatican line just as Communist parties follow the Moscow line.

The question of an ambassador at the Vatican has divided the nation and has raised serious problems for those charged with political decision. Protestants are troubled by the continuous pressure upon political leaders to grant a privilege that is upon a quid pro quo basis. As the late Archbishop Ryan, Roman Catholic Archbishop in Omaha, in frank statement put it:

"Though conscious of the religious power of the Pope, head of the Catholic Church, we [the people and the Government of the United States] have chosen to remain blind to the political power of the Pope, who is King. But is it the part of wisdom not to recognize the Papacy for what it is, despite any religious feelings to the contrary?" It is this very political power that has been and is being used to deny religious liberty that is of concern to Protestants. The Archbishop continued, "The diplomatic history of modern Europe presents few, if any, examples of complete unselfish relationships between nations. When nations act, they proceed on the well-known lines of quid pro quo. It is patently absurd to assume that Germany, France, and England now recognize the Vatican State for any high motives of Christian charity. If they give something, they expect something in return."

It is pertinent to ask, what did Hitler get in return? What did Mussolini get in return? Surely, whatever was given these dictators by the Vatican State must have been of some value to them. What the personal representative of the President of the United States to His Holiness, the Pope, may have gotten is not revealed in the correspondence that passed between the President and Mr. Myron C. Taylor. Certain it is that our representative got what the Pope decided he might have. If any religious leader anywhere has any information to give the United States Government, the way is open, and it is precisely the way that is open to the American churches, namely, the frank transmittal of information which the President of the United States may use as he sees fit. The President has full right to send a representative to anyone or to any place to secure information which will enable him to better serve the American people; but to appoint an individual with the rank of ambassador to the head of a church is to violate the principle of the separation of the Church and the State. That this was the first step toward a hoped-for diplomatic recognition of the Vatican is hardly open to question.

It is not the desire to be of spiritual service that underlies the demand for such an ambassador.

A careful reading of a scholarly volume published by the Catholic University Press, entitled, "United States Ministers to the Papal State, Instructions and Dispatches, 1848–1868," edited with Introduction by Leo Francis Stock, is pertinent in this connection.

One of the striking references on the first page of the Introduction is to the "liberal character of the reforms of the new Pontiff"—Pius X. The first reform listed is "his release of political prisoners." That was not in the Middle Ages. The year was 1846. In those days, the Vatican actually ruled a state, had its soldiers and its political prisoners. We now have the spectacle of ambassadors to a State that is really but a State in name, representing their states to a person who is really the head of a church. This is to obliterate the line that we believe should separate Church and State.

James Buchanan wrote to Lewis Cass, Jr., the representative at the Vatican in 1849, "It is only as a temporal Prince, exercising actual authority within his own Dominions, that the Government of the United States can have any relations with His Holiness." Technically, the Pope today is the head of a state. But Roman Catholics insist that it is merely form, it is not a state in the true sense of the term. Then why have diplomatic relations with the head of a church?

I quote again from Lewis R. Cass, our representative at the Vatican, in his letter to the Secretary of State, John M. Clayton, April 21, 1849. He speaks of the Roman population "among whom the desire is very strong to escape from the temporal domination of the Pope, not as Pope, but as Head of the College of Cardinals. . . . Communications have been made to me, from sources of the highest respectability, of the authority exercised by this ecclesiastical oligarchy, almost too monstrous for belief . . . being in complete possession of the courts of justice (if they deserve the name) and of the confessional, this body were enabled to convert all and every influence to their own personal and class aggrandizement, as they are accused of having done. In illustration of this system, I will quote from the law of fiducia, which is a matter of record, and familiar to every Roman. By this law, a dying man can give his property in trust to the priest attending his last moments, the secret words which the priest declares were uttered to him being considered his valid testament. Of course, such a law alone gives the priesthood the power of disinheriting any family and succeeding to any heritage."

I do not record these matters to criticize, but to make clear there is a reason why Church and State should be separate.

As Christianity faces the changing world, particularly in the Far East, the issue of religious liberty comes to the forefront. What of the future of Christian missions in China? As the years pass, what denials of religious liberty may be expected in the great state of Pakistan which is also a Moslem state? The guarantees written into the Constitution of India are highly significant, but if Christians expect these guarantees to be guarantees in fact, it is imperative that the Christian house itself be set in order and the principles that it enunciates be those that affirm religious liberty.

FOUR

The Social Service State and Serfdom

IN FEBRUARY, 1950, THREE HUNDRED EIGHTY-TWO DELEGATES
from thirty states, the District of Columbia, and Canada,
representing twenty-two religious denominations, met in The
National Study Conference on the Church and Economic Life
in Detroit. It was my honor to draft the original statement
which subsequently was considered by a small committee,
revised, and finally read to the Conference. It was then referred to a committee composed of nineteen members, among
them Mr. Noel Sargent, the Secretary of the National Association of Manufacturers; Mr. John L. Lovett, General Manager
of the Michigan Manufacturers Association; Mr. Al. White-
house, District Director of the United Steel Workers, CIO;
Dr. William Adams Brown, Jr. of the Brookings Institution;
Mr. Charles P. Taft of Cincinnati; Bishop Theodore Ludlow
of the Protestant Episcopal Church; and Dr. Raymond W.
Miller, Special Lecturer of the Harvard Graduate School of
Business Administration. This committee reached unanimous
decision upon the general statement which I, as chairman, read
to the Conference. This statement was adopted with but one

dissenting vote. Because of such close personal relationship to the statement, I feel free to quote at length from it.

The Gospel is concerned with all the activities of man, individual and social. Therefore, the Christian faith is relevant to the economic order. The Church, as the custodian of "the sacred and imperishable message of eternal salvation," is charged with a four-fold duty as Christians in fellowship confront the economic life. It must be the teacher of the principles of conduct; a voice of judgment; a guardian of moral and spiritual values already won; and the herald of a better day.

Christians judge all economic systems by the imperatives of the Christian faith; Christians must not identify any economic order with the Gospel. The Christian Gospel is not to be found in Adam Smith's *Wealth of Nations* nor in Karl Marx's *Capital*. It is to be found in Matthew, Mark, Luke, and John, in the Acts of the Apostles, the Epistles of the New Testament, and the vision of St. John in the Revelation. It is to be found in the preaching of the Hebrew prophets, in the lives of saints and martyrs, in the service of the faithful followers of Christ, and in the continuing revelation of God. That faith affirms the supreme worth of persons. Institutions must be tested finally by their contribution to the enrichment of personality.

. . . . . .

Christians acquainted with the centuries know that the struggle to emancipate the worker is part of the age-long resolve to lift man to the status of brother. Once the work of the world was done by slaves, but a brother in chains was a contradiction in terms. Slavery had to go. Serfdom was likewise brought under the judgment of God. Feudalism with its aristocracy and privilege gave way. The voice of democracy stirred the people to action with its insistence upon the rights of man, its denial of the divine right of kings, and its call for liberty, equality, and fraternity. Into the midst of this revolutionary surge came the industrial revolution. Handicraft industry was superseded by the factory system. The worker had ceased to be slave or serf. He had become a free man, free to sell his own labor where he himself determined. A mistaken conception was prevalent that the unrestricted play of self-interest would in the long run mean social well-being. Laborers in factory and on farm, subjected to exploitation, sought to protect their interest by organizing labor unions. These were at first regarded as conspiracies and ruthlessly suppressed. In the course of the years, the right to organize was won, the worker became more powerful, and the democratic principle was introduced into the work-life. Meanwhile, ever widening research, the development of technology, the genius of management, the skill of labor, and a growing sense of social responsibility resulted in amazing advances.

But man is still exploited by his brother. Vast inequalities in wealth and therefore in status, fundamental differences in scales of value, and wide disparities in the possession of power create and maintain class consciousness. Class is a concept too small to unite men for social emancipation. Upon the basis of class, all that can be done is to make one class ready to fight another class. Man needs a larger unifying concept. It is found in the Christian ideal of brotherhood under the Fatherhood of God and the Christian teaching of the solidarity of the human family.

Time is of the essence. Principles that mean both unity and justice must be applied soon enough to turn man from the battlefield of class conflict to the cooperative avenues of peaceful progress. The fratricidal struggle of class war upon a world scale must be avoided.

The Christian knows that the Kingdom of God cannot be built upon foundations of economic injustice. He refuses to acquiesce in those inequalities that deny equal opportunity. Equality of consideration does not necessarily mean identity of treatment. The American lives in one of the freest lands upon the earth. His pursuit of happiness under the conditions of liberty has enriched life. Significant advances have been made in equalizing opportunity and further advances are possible and imperative, but when all such socially controllable inequalities have been removed, there will remain sources of conflict that root in the sinfulness and greed of the human heart. The primary task of the Christian therefore continues to be one of evangelism in which the individual accepts Jesus Christ as Lord and Saviour, becomes a new man in Christ

[83]

Jesus, and moves out in cooperation with his fellow Christians to build an economic life more in accord with the will of God as revealed in Christ. The Gospel is not an opiate; it is, when applied, a regenerating force capable of transforming economic relations into a fellowship and the individual into a brother.

. . . . . .

If man is exploited by man, that becomes an issue of graver import to the theistic Christian than to the atheistic communist. Unfortunately, masses of mankind think that communism is more opposed to the "exploitation of man by man" than is Christianity. They are wrong. No true Christian is complacent in the face of periodic crises in which millions are denied work, consumers' needs are unmet, and unemployment becomes epidemic. Unemployed men, idle machines, and unused materials present at the same time and place do not make sense to men endowed with God-given reason. Christian principles must be translated into concrete measures expressive of the Christian ideal. This is a task for stewards whose economic insights, executive ability, and research skills are regarded as a sacred trust. Means must be discovered with which to realize moral ends.

. . . . . .

The Christian must face up to the issues that are involved both in free enterprise and in adequate planning for the common good. There is a planning that does mean serfdom. There is a planning that does contribute to freedom. The freedom that enables private enterprise itself to plan must be preserved; but the freedom must be maintained that is essential to democratic decisions in which the people through their government, plan, for example, for public education and health, conservation of natural resources, fiscal and foreign policy, national defense, cooperation in international bodies, as well as control of monopolies and restraint of antisocial individuals and groups.

The challenge to free enterprise that lies in monopoly must be considered. Selfishness seldom thinks beyond immediate interests, and cannot be relied upon to plan for the well-being of future generations or for the conservation of natural resources. Freedom

[84]

must be interpreted to include freedom for all men, the strong and the weak, the talented and the handicapped; and such freedom involves clear distinction between the planning that enslaves and the planning that emancipates.

I

British labor demands the universal enforcement of a national minimum standard of life. Is this a reasonable objective, or is it the enunciation of an unrealizable, utopian proposal? In the light of the principles laid down in the general Statement to the Detroit Conference, is provision for the welfare of a nation's children part of the planning that enslaves or the planning that emancipates? When Christians talk about the right to be well-born, the right to a home, the right to an education, the right to work, and the right to leisure, in how far do they justify the guarantee of such rights by the State?

Difficult questions emerge from any consideration of planning. If, for instance, the United States of America is determined that every child shall have the right to an education, in other words, plans for the education of its children, should the nation plan likewise for the health of its children? In the first instance, property owners are taxed to maintain the public educational system. Should people be taxed in similar fashion to provide health service for all the people, or at least for the young? If the answer is yes, how far does one go in such reasoning? The declaration that the essentials should be provided socially appears at first to be the proclamation of a moral principle, but does this mean that food and clothing should be provided socially? If so, who makes the decisions as to what kind of food and what kind of clothing? Is it not true that there is a line beyond which the community cannot go in meeting the welfare needs of the people without so limiting their freedom as to bring serfdom?

Professor F. A. Hayek, in a thoughtful study of this issue

entitled "The Road to Serfdom," argued that socialist measures call for more socialist measures, and in the long run liberty is lost and serfdom is the lot of the common people. Barbara Wootton, on the contrary, in "Freedom Under Planning," analyzes the concept of freedom with care, and insists that *"Freedom* has to be perpetually reinterpreted into *freedoms.* You can philosophize endlessly about freedom," she says, "but in daily life it is freedoms that you want. . . . Freedom may be simply defined as ability to do what you want. . . . Freedom means freedom to do what I want, and not what anybody else wants me to want—or else it has no meaning at all. . . . So far as freedom is concerned, what people want to do must be taken as something to be discovered, not changed." Naturally, she holds that, "Freedom for everybody to do what he wants is not necessarily the sole purpose of organized society. There may be other admirable social ends which conflict with, or demand limitations upon, freedom."

It is quite possible to have a society in which the individual may be well fed, well housed, well clad, and even well entertained, and yet be a slave. I once saw a photograph that to me was even more shocking than the terrifying photographs that were taken when I stood beside the stack of naked bodies piled before the crematorium in the frightful concentration camp of Buchenwald. In this photograph, also revelatory of Nazi tyranny, several men of splendid physique were bathing beneath the showers. Standing nearby was a Nazi guard. These men were well fed. They were cared for with the solicitude that characterizes a farmer who is making hogs ready for market. They were to be used by the Nazis for heavy work, and were, for the present, necessary. Except for freedom and the recognition of their infinite worth, they possessed about all that any welfare state could give.

Is it true that the democratic state cannot provide social services without destroying the freedom of the citizen?

The Social Service State and Serfdom

When the Constitution of the United States was drafted, our forefathers declared that one of its primary objects was to "promote the general welfare." It is an interesting fact that these far-seeing and patriotic men believed that the people could "form a more perfect union, establish justice, insure domestic tranquility, provide for the common defense" as well as "promote the general welfare" and, at the same time, "secure the blessings of liberty." They believed they could do that for themselves and likewise for their posterity.

Unfortunately, the issue that lies in such terms as "planning," "the welfare state," "the social service state," and the like, has become a matter of partisan politics, and is therefore fought about rather than thought about. An intelligent man would rather be hungry and free than well fed and enslaved. The religious leaders at Detroit declared, "There is a planning that does mean serfdom. There is a planning that does contribute to freedom."

In a series of interesting little volumes in which Stuart Chase reports to the Twentieth Century Fund, he considered in 1942 "The Road We Are Traveling" and, a little later, "Goals for America: A Budget of Our Needs and Resources." Four additional volumes completed the series. Mr. Chase states, "The old patterns were based on the theory of *laissez faire,* in which nobody is charged with seeing the economy as a whole." He considers the standards for community survival in the post-war world, and lists four of them: "(1) The first consideration will be adequate military protection; (2) the complete, final and utter abolition of chronic unemployment; (3) the establishment of minimum standards of well being for the entire population; and (4) to hold natural resources at par so far as is physically possible." In this connection, he points out that a nation which "runs through its soils, forests, grass lands, watersheds, minerals, is certain to face a terrible day of reckoning. Here is one department where a modern nation can really go bankrupt." Mr. Chase quotes Walter D. Fuller, President of the Curtis Publishing Company and chairman of the Board of the National Association of Manufacturers, as follows:

One thing is certain, the people of this country are fighting this war for a better world in which to live. They would like to get it through democracy, liberty and free enterprise. But they are determined to have this better world of greater security one way or another, and if they don't get it through present principles they will look elsewhere.

The handwriting is on the wall. We either must cut the cloth to fit the pattern or the reformers and demagogues will. We can point to past accomplishments of free enterprise until hell freezes over, but people are concerned about the future, not the past.

This country cannot return to the "good old days" after this war, because those days just weren't good enough. They were the days when 28 million people were receiving some form of public assistance; when there were 10 million unemployed; when there was want amidst plenty. They were the days of idle money, idle men and idle plants. . . . Even in 1929, there were more than 42 families in 100 with incomes less than $25 a week.[1]

II

Can these goals be realized without planning? Can we keep our freedom, if we do plan?

In "The Road We Are Traveling, 1914–1942," Mr. Chase sets forth the reasons why "back to business as usual" is impossible. He points out that any attempt to break up the American Telephone and Telegraph Company into small competing units would result in loss, not gain. He regards the giant corporations and cartels as the natural culmination of our system, rather than "in effect, a denial of the system." He then

[1] "Goals for America" by Stuart Chase, pp. 19–20. Twentieth Century Fund, New York, 1942.

points out that something which he cannot designate by a name and therefore calls "X" is displacing the system of free enterprise all over the world, and lists certain of the characteristics of "X":

A strong, centralized government.

An executive arm growing at the expense of the legislative and judicial arms. In some countries, power is consolidated in a dictator, issuing decrees.

The control of banking, credit and security exchanges by the government.

The underwriting of employment by the government, either through armaments or public works.

The underwriting of social security by the government—old age pensions, mothers' pensions, unemployment insurance, and the like.

The underwriting of food, housing and medical care by the government. The United States is already experimenting with providing these essentials. Other nations are far along the road.

The use of the deficit spending technique to finance these underwritings. The annually balanced budget has lost its old-time sanctity.

The abandonment of gold in favor of managed currencies.

The control of foreign trade by the government, with increasing emphasis on bilateral agreements and barter deals.

The control of natural resources, with increasing emphasis on self-sufficiency.

The control of energy sources—hydroelectric power, coal, petroleum, natural gas.

The control of transportation—railway, highway, airway, waterway.

The control of agricultural production.

The control of labor organizations, often to the point of prohibiting strikes.

The enlistment of young men and women in youth corps devoted to health, discipline, community service and ideologies consistent with those of the authorities. The CCC camps have just inaugurated military drill.

Heavy taxation, with especial emphasis on the estates and incomes of the rich.

Not much "taking over" of property or industries in the old socialistic sense. The formula appears to be *control without ownership*. It is interesting to recall that the same formula is used by the management of great corporations in depriving stockholders of power.

The state control of communications and propaganda.[2]

Professor Hayek would call a halt to these changes which today are looked upon with suspicion both by many old time Socialists and also by present advocates of the free economy.

George B. Galloway and Associates, in perhaps the most scholarly consideration of the issue of planning, entitled "Planning for America," say that we must "plan or perish." They hold that "American planning stems from at least four native American sources: from the planning movement in American cities; from the conservation movement in natural resources, which dates back to the early years of this century and owes its inception to the efforts of Theodore Roosevelt and Gifford Pinchot; from the scientific management or industrial engineering movement in American industry fathered by Frederick W. Taylor; and from the contribution of the social sciences to an understanding of human institutions, values, and activities." They point out that, "Social planning may be distinguished from individual planning and from plans designed to protect group or sectional interests. Social planning centralizes responsibility for the organization of production, whereas individual planning decentralizes it in the spontaneous decisions of private citizens which are supposed to conduce to the general welfare. . . . There is no more regimentation . . . in executing planning than unplanned operations. For compulsion is present in either case:

[2] "The Road We Are Traveling, 1914–1942" by Stuart Chase, pp. 95–96. The Twentieth Century Fund, 1942.

the compulsion of chance or that of plan. . . . In the technical sense of the term given by engineering and industry, social planning needs an institutional mind capable of thinking in terms of experience larger than that which comes to any individual; able to define distant goals, to devise efficient ways and means of attaining them and to pursue these remote ends consistently yet with a flexibility that permits adjustment to changing conditions." They then add, "Like any technology, planning is politically and ethically neutral. . . . Thus planning may be used by any form of society in pursuit of its own ends, be they national power or human welfare." Galloway declares, "It is the aim of modern planning to implement the plans of private enterprise and to supplement them, where necessary, by public activity." Critics of such planning insist that public enterprises have a tendency to become ends in themselves, that the personnel necessary to manage such enterprise becomes a bureaucracy that inevitably seeks to defend its area of control. Some speak of the "tyrant state" and hold that tyranny is the inevitable port of the ship that embarks upon the seas of planning. Galloway writes as a scientist, and outlines four fields of planning—physical planning, economic planning, social planning, and cultural planning. These he describes, as follows:

Thus the practitioners of physical planning set forth their aims as (1) the conservation and efficient use of natural resources; (2) the effective location of economic and social units (adjustment of site to function): roads, power lines, schools, communities; (3) a coordinated transport system related to the physical characteristics of the country as well as to economic and social needs; (4) the maintenance of a suitable natural environment for the development of wholesome forms of outdoor recreation; and (5) the preservation of esthetic values in the landscape.

Economic planners state their objectives to be: (1) a progressively rising standard of living, including minimum essentials for all at all times; (2) maximum utilization of our productive powers to increase output so as to make a rise in standard of living possible; (3) the adoption to this end of policies of expansion rather than restriction by industry, labor, and government; such policies to be based in turn upon scientific methods of increasing efficiency, productivity, and distribution; (4) the reduction of industrial fluctuations and the maintenance of a balance between production and consumption; (5) an increase of, and greater equality in the distribution of, the national income; (6) greater stability of employment and continuity of income; (7) greater interest and satisfaction in work; and (8) a reduction in the hours of labor.

Meanwhile, social planners are seeking better physical health, lower infant mortality, and abolition of child labor; better housing for the masses and improved home surroundings; larger educational facilities; opportunity for active and wholesome recreation; and the reduction of crime to a minimum. While cultural planners formulate their objectives in terms of an increase and wider distribution of scientific organizations to increase a scientific attitude of mind among the people; wider and better facilities for bringing to the people opportunities for the enjoyment of the arts; efforts to help develop a greater sense of play and art; and facilities for developing a greater variety of social and cultural interests in all groups of the people.[3]

One highly significant sentence from Dr. Galloway must be recorded. He says, "Whatever the aims, agreement upon the ends of social life, some general consensus of national purpose, a common vision of the American ideal, is essential to national planning in war or peace." It is quite true, as he argues, that "American planning, if it is to be consistent with American ideals, must be democratic in method, following democratic processes and seeking social objectives determined by majority rule. These processes involve freedom of citizens through representative institutions in government and industry to propose, discuss, and decide on policies and measures,

[3] "Planning for America," George B. Galloway and Associates, p. 10. Henry Holt and Co., 1941.

and continuously to reexamine and appraise their results."

The Constitution itself is a plan. Leaders who insist that free enterprise is as essential a freedom as is civil liberty often forget that such a statement is in effect a goal and that proper steps must be taken to insure the maintenance of free enterprise, in other words, planning is necessary for free enterprise as well as for collective enterprise.

Miss Wootton states the case for freedom under planning, but admits that planning is "the conscious and deliberate choice of economic priorities by some public authority," and sees the heart of the matter in the planning of production. It is precisely this that many hold will destroy initiative, introduce the dead hand of bureaucracy, and finally end freedom. Miss Wootton holds that "uncoördinated, small-scale plans of individuals generally add up to a result that is completely unplanned; and the large-scale planning of private monopolies raises issues which, although alarming and important enough, are different from those characteristic of what is coming to be called a 'planned economic system.' " She thinks planning is a matter of degree, but competent students hold that price controls, for instance, call for supplementary controls that after a time may mean complete control. There is a fundamental distinction between the state's planning priorities in production and socialism, since socialism involves the collective ownership as well as the democratic management, and thus the operation of industry. But is this distinction as significant as the planners believe? The divorce of ownership from management has placed new power, and therefore control, in managers. The question of who owns the stock certificate is not as important as once it was.

There are many kinds of freedom, such as civil, cultural, political, economic, and religious freedom. Discussions in this field should consider the impact of planning upon the particular freedom under consideration. Can we continue to control those to whom we delegate power for the purpose of planning, or do the controls or collective enterprises established become so powerful in themselves that democratic control in itself is jeopardized?

The fact that power corrupts means that tyranny is always potentially present wherever power is held, unless the control of the people is so clear and so easy to exercise that delegations of power can be modified or withdrawn. The danger of tyranny is ever present.

In a sense, the formulation of a Bill of Rights is, in itself, planning. We plan for the rights of individuals. Professor Hayek holds that economic planning "inevitably brings the worst to the top." If this be true, further discussion is of no value, since this thesis discredits democracy itself. Since the individual citizen is at the receiving end of the benefits as well as of the burdens of planning, he, given proper opportunity in the democratic process to express himself, is in a position to be a corrective and controlling force. Beneath all of this discussion lies a religious question, namely, can religion develop people who say "we" oftener than they say "I," or "they."

One of the most thoughtful books of recent years is "The Future Economic Policy of the United States," by William Adams Brown, Jr., now of the Brookings Institution in Washington. He states, "But of one thing there can be no doubt. The American people will never again feel that in economic matters they are the helpless victims of events. They know that they have alternatives to mass unemployment and social injustice, and that in economic matters they can and will be masters of their fate." This is but another way of saying that unemployed men, idle machines, and unused material present at the same time and place do not make sense to people who have conquered a continent and built a civilization within a century. The American people possess the resources and the

[94]

creative ability to bring men, machine, and materials together. Dr. Brown writes from the point of view of one who is convinced by facts that the free enterprise system makes a greater contribution to freedom and to personality than does any other economic system known to man. He insists that:

No amount of skill in administration or flexibility in negotiation can eliminate the hard core of ultimate choice that faces the nation. The essential principle of opportunity cost cannot be amended. We must forego something to obtain any worthwhile economic or social objective.

America cannot have both security of occupations and unlimited private initiative.

It cannot have both unlimited freedom to pursue *any* domestic economy policy it wants, and the advantages of a working world economy.

It cannot have a free enterprise system and *no* business fluctuations.

It cannot have an export surplus in *all* its international accounts. It cannot, with limited resources, satisfy the maximum economic aspirations of *all* its citizens.

Those who hold out to the people the prospect of an age of plenty in which no one will suffer for his economic mistakes, or because some interest greater than his own must be saved, do not make a blueprint for the future, but present a utopia under the guise of prediction.

We must calculate the price to be paid for the life we want. Dr. Brown argues that "Thoughtful Americans are searching for the answer to the question whether we can proceed farther along the road of modifying our traditional economic system without sacrificing it altogether." He defines the free enterprise system, as follows: "A formal definition of the free enterprise system is one in which final decisions as to the allocation of resources are made by private entrepreneurs—the risk-taking managers—who seek to maximise their profits and who respond to the dictates of the consumer expressed through

[95]

demand in the market." That monopoly interferes with this concept of free enterprise is self-evident. Management and ownership have been divorced. Economies in production are not automatically passed to the consumer. Breaches in the free enterprise system have occurred, and these were made first, as Dr. Brown insists, by private interests. In a word, "the first economic planners were business men."

Mr. Henry R. Luce, from time to time, discusses what he calls welfare capitalism. He argues that all of the benefits that men seek by way of the welfare state can be had under the capitalist system. He believes it is necessary to maintain the freedom of this system in order to produce the goods necessary for the abundant life that man desires. He does not believe such productivity is possible under the so-called planned economies. The latter stifle creativity, production drops off, and the economy stagnates. I once heard Mr. Luce say, in substance, "Maintain the system, then tax us as you please in order to pay for the social services that may be necessary." The difficulty, however, lies in the fact that those who are to be taxed seldom accept taxation graciously. If they possess certain controls in the media used to determine public opinion, these media are apt to be used not for the purpose of securing the necessary taxes for the necessary social services, but rather to block all attempts to secure such taxes.

It is a striking and significant fact that no great social reform has been sponsored by American business. Within the ranks of American business are the ablest executives, organizers, and engineers in the world. Our leaders have revealed genius in mastering the problems of production. Motion pictures taken from a plane flying at low altitude over the great industrial centers of America would reveal an industrial plant second to none in the world, efficiency unequaled, and planning, under freedom, unsurpassed. The genius of American leadership must be directed to the problems now confronting the nation as a whole, in fact, the world. These are problems of distribution, of social justice. They are the problems that inhere in the determination to translate the ethical ideals of religion into the realities of the common life. Such problems could be solved, I believe, by men whose abilities have made American enterprise the wonder as well as the envy of the world. If there could be less energy spent in propagandizing the nation under the slogan, "Liberty versus Socialism," and more intelligence given to the solution of the problems referred to, free enterprise would be maintained and justice established.

There are those who insist that the self-interest essential to effective competition so conditions men who participate in competition that they cannot give themselves to those endeavors that enrich the commonwealth. This I doubt, for the reason that many of the leaders who would be most completely conditioned, if this theory were true, are the very men who have established the great charitable foundations that in turn have brought untold wealth to the community.

It is unfortunately true that the leadership required is spent in attacking those who call for justice instead of in creating the conditions of justice. American business has not only failed to sponsor a major social reform, but, unfortunately, has fought most reforms. It fought the fight of labor to organize. It fought the demand for an eight-hour day. It fought plans for workingmen's insurance and compensation for accidents. It fought the attempts to regulate the abuses of railroad rebates. It refused to admit that there is a public interest in certain public utilities. It fought the regulation of the stock exchange. It has fought attempts of the people to serve themselves, as in parcel post or in the Tennessee Valley.

Of course, a great case can be made for the achievements of American enterprise, and it can be argued that the rising standard of living is due to our economic system. It can be argued that large numbers of social benefits flow almost automatically from the system and that, indirectly, therefore, men who have given themselves to the maintenance of free enterprise and to the solution of the problems of production have, in effect, been social reformers. This is beside the point. The issues that are before us must be faced. The people will not again tolerate widespread unemployment. It will not do to speak of the "business cycle." Men cannot eat business cycles, nor can they live on stock certificates and other evidences of wealth when depression, which some regard as beneficent, restores equilibrium to the economic life. Mr. Luce's plea for a welfare capitalism makes great appeal, but the words must unbend, must leave the offices of *Time, Life,* and *Fortune* and move into the communities with welfare in their hands. Religious thinkers doubt that enlightened selfishness is a motive that will create welfare capitalism. Railroads object to subsidies for aviation, and farmers oppose expenditures for public health in urban communities because the amount available for crop subsidies is thereby reduced. Labor objects to a Reconstruction Finance Corporation, but favors laws that in turn benefit labor. Publishers fight attempts of the Post Office to charge a sufficient amount to pay for the handling and delivery of magazines and newspapers. The case is argued back and forth on a partisan basis, rather than in the interest of the common good. Bertrand Russell once said that if the temperature of our homes were to be regulated by government, there would be one party insisting upon the boiling point as proper and another party calling for the freezing point as necessary.

Much of the discussion is a defense of present practice rather than consideration of possible services under freedom in the interest of equality. The President of the Sante Fe Railroad published a brochure comparing the number of men who work upon the British Railroads in different categories with those who work on the Sante Fe. The fact that England is densely populated and that the Santa Fe pulls long trains over unpopulated areas makes such comparison valueless. The president assumes that the number of employees today is large because of a Socialist Britain, without checking the number of employees when the railroads of Britain were privately owned.

It is time that the air be cleared and the issue faced upon a higher plane than that of selfishness. Contemporary attacks upon government is discrediting the government in the mind of the populace. The people are in danger of forgetting that the representatives in Washington are the representatives of the people. They may overlook the fact that it is our government and that we ourselves are basically responsible. One of the essential conditions of revolution is a discredited government. Men who raise doubts in the minds of the people relative to the integrity of government in order to hide their own lobbying activities through which they seek special privilege are themselves in danger of becoming subversive.

III

The Church must not be caught in contemporary confusion. Much of the argument is beside the point. The realities must be faced. Christianity here, as elsewhere, brings practices to judgment. Totalitarianism is far more likely to emerge in societies where free men have failed to build the practices of righteousness than to result from the social services of a community that has resolved democratically to create the conditions of justice. If we can frame a bill of civil rights, is there any reason why we cannot frame a bill of economic rights? The National Resources Planning Board attempted to do this, and set down the following propositions:

1. The right to work, usefully and creatively through the productive years;
2. The right to fair pay, adequate to command the necessities and amenities of life in exchange for work, ideas, thrift, and other socially valuable service;

[99]

3. The right to adequate food, clothing, shelter, and medical care;
4. The right to security, with freedom from fear of old age, want, dependency, sickness, unemployment, and accident.
5. The right to live in a system of free enterprise, free from compulsory labor, irresponsible private power, arbitrary public authority, and unregulated monopolies;
6. The right to come and go, to speak or to be silent, free from the spyings of secret political police;
7. The right to equality before the law, with equal access to justice in fact;
8. The right to education, for work, for citizenship, and for personal growth and happiness; and
9. The right to rest, recreation, and adventure, the opportunity to enjoy life and take part in an advancing civilization.

Man properly demands fearless leisure and fruitful labor. Debate may follow as to the best means of realizing the rights enumerated above and in achieving leisure without fear and labor that is productive. We have thought of the State in negative terms. We have insisted that it is to act as an umpire, to fix the rules, to say no. But can we not think of the State in positive terms, a State that can say yes and that can take steps to achieve worthy ends for the people? Wise men will avoid the centralization that means inefficiency, bureaucracy, and the denials of liberty. They will insist upon the practices of decentralization and of decisions, as well as responsibility, close to those who are served.

The truth is we do not live in a system of free enterprise or of collective enterprise. Professor R. H. Tawney commented facetiously upon the situation in the United States, as follows:

I remember a delightful visit to the West of America. After passing some weeks in a State-owned park, and driving through fifty miles of State-owned forests, I crossed a river on a public ferry, and after traveling some distance on a municipal tram, was conducted over the civic electric works, the tax-supported hospital and the public schools, tried in vain to obtain refreshment at several saloons, which had been closed without compensation by the State; and finally visited the State University, where I heard a professor of economics, whose salary was defrayed from public funds, deliver to a body of several hundred students, whose fees were paid from the same source, a lecture on the importance of untrammeled private enterprise and the dangerous immorality of Socialism. As I listened with awe to his statement of principles— eloquent, lucid and intimidating—I recalled the answer of a London school child to a question addressed to her as to the use of certain common objects of daily life. "What," she was asked, "are pins for?" "Pins," she replied, "are very useful things. They have saved many people's lives by not a-swallowing of them." [4]

Millions of people are engaged in socially necessary service rendered by the municipality, the state, the nation. Our system of highways is collectively owned. The public schools of America are one of our greatest achievements. Anyone who will call the roll, from the public health service to the military, from the lighthouses that guard our shores to the fire departments that protect our homes, from the Bureau of Standards to the Reclamation Service, from the research in the Department of Agriculture to the services of the Farm Agent, from the Port Authorities of New York, with their tunnels under the Hudson, to the National Parks, knows perfectly well that there are vast public services rendered by the people to the people, and we are not enslaved by them. Does anyone wish toll roads? Is there any man who would turn the Post Office over to some private corporation? Does a visitor to the docks who notes the metal discs upon the hawsers object to a public health service that protects the nation from bubonic plague? Are the safety measures of a Civil Aeronautics Board the shackles that enslave free men?

To ask such questions is to answer them. There is a proper and necessary place for the social service state. It does not have to become the omni-competent state. It need not become a

[4] "The British Labor Movement." Yale University Press, 1925, pp. 172–173.

tyrant state. Journalists who have announced themselves as authorities upon "The Road Ahead" make themselves ridiculous when, advertising their own competence as economists, they speak of the "mixed economy" as nonsense. Religious leaders approach this issue in terms of principle. They insist upon the worth of persons. They affirm the supreme value of personality. They therefore do not ask, Is it Capitalist? Is it Socialist? Is it Communist? They ask, Is it Christian? By that they mean, Does a particular way of getting a job done enrich personality, maintain freedom, release creative initiative, benefit humanity?

For instance, the religious leadership of the United States, I think, would generally agree that in the overwhelming percentage of American enterprise, free enterprise, as we call it, gives evidence of making greater contribution to personality than does any other economic system. They, therefore, stand for such freedom and such practice. But this is not to label all other services of government or of public corporations as socialism. It is rather to use such means as are most likely to lift life to higher levels. Consequently, when churchmen enter the Tennessee Valley and find a public corporation developing all of the resources of the Valley in the unity with which nature endowed the Valley, when they see that the rivers have been brought under control, proper provision made for navigation, the dams built and power developed, when they note that the mountains have been reforested, soil erosion has been brought to an end and, what is more important, soul erosion considered, they reach the conclusion that, in all probability, in the Tennessee Valley a public corporation so conceived and so serving is better for the people, makes a greater contribution to life, than would a private corporation developing power efficiently for the benefit of the stockholders. They stand, therefore, for the development of similar public corporations in many of the great valleys of the nation. The decision is made in terms of personality. When they note the deserts, and are aware that their reclamation is unattractive to private capital, they turn to the collective answer, and are proud of a bureau that has brought back hundreds of thousands of acres to production, that has opened up farms for free men who will own them privately. They may study a situation such as the damming up of the Colorado River, and may reach the conclusion that it is better to build the dam collectively, to name it after a great individualist, than it is to allow the Southern California Edison Company to own it and thus control the economic life of Southern California.

In a word, instead of approaching these issues with the dogmatism of the Capitalist, the dogmatism of the Communist, or the dogmatism of the Socialist, they move in upon them in terms of the religion of Jesus. They are not fearful of slogans. They are determined to maintain freedom, but to use that freedom scientifically for the realization of moral ends and the setting up of justice.

Detroit therefore said:

As Christians, we seek a society of freedom, order, justice, and fraternity in which men pursuing such basic values are continually open to the transforming influence of God's grace.

We seek a dynamic, *free* society in which there is opportunity to agree and disagree on many important goals for society and the means of achieving them; a society also in which people find their fullest freedom in the use of their liberties to increase the freedoms of others.

We seek an *orderly* society in which individuals and groups will use those social controls which will aid in stabilizing the economy at levels of employment providing work opportunities for all ready, able, and willing to work, and so increasing standards of living.

We seek a *just* society in which the common good is recognized as best served when individuals realize fully their responsibility for productive effort in the interests of society. In such a society

Christians will seek to make its benefits available as widely as possible, especially among its exposed and depressed citizens, as well as to reward individuals for their productive effort.

We seek a *fraternal* society in which God's will that we love one another as brothers is expressed in a mutuality of sacrifice and service, and by an awareness that in an interdependent economy the needs and interests of others are as important as our own.

We seek also a *productive* society in which our resources are efficiently utilized in the service of these values.

. . . . . .

There are two extreme positions taken as to the best economic policy for our society in the major areas of our economy: (a) the establishment of what is assumed to be an unregulated price system; (b) the planning and allocating of resources and the setting of prices and production by public authorities in key areas. The present economy conforms to neither position. There are various positions taken between these two extremes. We seek the use of a price system which has been strengthened in its operation and corrected in its abuses through various social controls. Some of the most crucial social controls are in the area of stabilizing incomes through regulation of the volume of money in the economy and of governmental taxes and expenditures. Christians and church groups seeking to educate people to take responsible economic action should understand these areas of our economy and clarify for themselves the action they believe ought to be taken to best serve such values as freedom and justice in these areas.

. . . . . .

We would favor making the bulk of our economic decisions as to allocation of resources and the production and distribution of commodities through a price system whose functions are discharged by private individuals and economic groups; but proper decisions and institutional arrangements need to be worked out in at least three areas in keeping with the basic values of justice and fraternity: (1) economic stabilization; (2) income distribution; (3) monopoly and power group control.[5]

[5] From "The Responsibility of Christians in an Interdependent Economic World," the Report of the Detroit Conference, pages 15-17.

FIVE

Christian Strategy in the Light of the World Crisis

STRATEGY DEALS WITH WHAT, WHEN, WHERE. TACTICS CONsiders How. In General Marshall's extraordinary report entitled, "The Winning of the War in Europe and the Pacific," the first chapter is entitled, "The Strategic Concept."

The World Council of Churches in session at Amsterdam in 1948 declared: "The evident demand of God in this situation is that the whole church should set itself to the total task of winning the whole world for Christ." This, like the underlying objective in General Marshall's chapter, is the bold strategic concept—the mission of the church.

When General Eisenhower was selected as the Supreme Allied Commander for Overlord he received the following directive, "You will enter the Continent of Europe and, in conjunction with the other Allied Nations, undertake operations aimed at the heart of Germany and the destruction of her armed forces." Amsterdam asked a critical question, and in its answer are revealed positions that must be taken if the

Church is some day to report to its Supreme Commander, "Mission accomplished."

The Protestant and Orthodox leaders present at Amsterdam faced the current situation as realistically as military men confront the positions and strength of the enemy and evaluate the men, materiel, and morale of their own forces.

I

Amsterdam asked, "What does the world see, or think it sees when it looks at the Church?"

The answer comes clear and courageous:

It is a Church divided, and in its separated parts are often found hesitancy, complacency, or the desire to domineer.

It is a Church that has largely lost touch with the dominant realities of modern life, and still tries to meet the modern world with language and a technique that may have been appropriate two hundred years ago.

It is a Church that, by its failure to speak effectively on the subject of war, has appeared impotent to deal with the realities of the human situation.

It is a Church accused by many of having been blind to the movement of God in history, of having sided with the vested interests of society and state, and of having failed to kindle the vision and to purify the wills of men in a changing world.

It is a Church under suspicion in many quarters of having used its missionary enterprise to further the foreign policies of state and the imperialistic designs of the powers of the West.

The very fact that leaders were willing to face the current situation realistically is evidence of strength. Whenever an institution is unwilling to consider criticism from outside and to impose rigorous self-criticism upon itself, it evidences weakness.

Of course, these leaders were aware of the fact that much

of this indictment might be untrue, but the facts forced them to say, "The Church is called to deep shame and penitence for its failure to manifest Jesus Christ to men as He really is."

Quite properly, Amsterdam estimated the reserves of the Church, its capacity to conquer in the Name of Christ. The Assembly declared:

Yet the Church is still the Church of God, in which, and in which alone, He is pleased to reveal Himself and His redemptive purpose in Jesus Christ, in Whom, and in Whom alone, the renewal of man's life is possible. It is a Church to which, through the upheavals of the modern world, God cries aloud and says, "Come, let us reason together."

It is a Church that is, to millions of faithful people, the place where they receive the grace of Christ and are given the strength to live with the power of His victory.

It is a Church awaking to its great opportunity to enter as the minister of the redemption wrought by Christ into that world with which God has confronted us.

It is a Church that today desires to treat evangelism as the common task of all the churches, and transcends the traditional distinction between the so-called Christian and so-called non-Christian lands.

In planning the over-all strategy of the Church, the counts of the critical indictment courageously uttered at Amsterdam must be considered.

Unfortunately, it is "a Church divided."

II

The first principle of over-all strategy is to heal its divisions.
There is far greater unity within Protestantism than is generally realized. In the United States, critics who stress the fragmented nature of Protestantism declare there are 256 religious denominations. That is true. It is also true that there are 13 religious communions, each one of which has a million

[107]

members or more. In the 13 will be found 82% of all the
church membership of the nation. There are 55 communions
that have 50,000 members or more. In the 55 will be found
97.4% of the total church membership of the United States.
In other words, in the 201 remaining groups there are but
2.6% of the total membership. This is not to discount small-
ness. Some of the smallest of the communions have made
highly significant spiritual contributions—for instance, the
Quakers. There are many, and I am one of them, who would
prefer 256 separate communions to one large communion if
that involved hierarchy, the denial of diversity in unity, the
rejection of decentralization, and abrogation of the practice
of the democratic principle of consent. The large number of
communions is due to the very fact of the religious liberty
that exists in America. The creative contributions of smaller
groups must never be discounted by those who would heal
our divisions. Dean Luther A. Weigle of Yale University in
"The Challenge of the Future" presents significant statistical
tables.[1]

He reports families rather than communions, and thus lists
eleven bodies.

DENOMINATION	BODIES	MEMBERS
Roman Catholic	1	23,419,791
Baptist	23	14,207,775
Methodist	20	10,629,280
Lutheran	20	5,129,147
Jewish	1	4,641,184
Presbyterian	10	2,933,768
Protestant Episcopal	1	2,227,524
Disciples	2	1,981,905
Congregational	1	1,075,401
Mormon	7	987,315
Reformed	4	979,388
Eleven denominational families	90	68,212,478
Other denominations	166	4,280,191
All denominations	256	72,492,669

[1] "The Challenge of the Future" in *Methodism*, edited by William K. Anderson, copyright, 1947, by Stone and Pierce.

Stated in percentages, this listing shows that the eleven families of denominations have 94 per cent of the total church membership of the country, leaving to 166 other denominations only 6 per cent. The figures are:

Eight Protestant familes	54	per cent
Roman Catholic	33.3	per cent
Jewish	6.4	per cent
Mormon	1.3	per cent
Eleven denominational families	94	per cent
Other denominations	6	per cent
All denominations	100	per cent

The Federal Council of the Churches of Christ in America is another expression of unity. The Federal Council is the churches themselves in coöperation at the national level. Twenty-seven great communions, Protestant and Orthodox, are one in this coöperation, and within the membership of the 27 denominations, so coöperating, will be found 29,000,000 members. Similar councils in other lands to a greater or lesser degree evidence similar coöperation.

The World Council itself is the outstanding example of coöperative enterprise since it brings together 151 denominations, Protestant, Orthodox, Anglican and Old Catholic, and at the world level makes possible coöperation of first importance. Many believe that in the very fact of working together the trend toward union will be accelerated and that from this coöperation may come the eventual reunion of the churches. The World Council of Churches is not a church. That is clearly stated in its constitution and other authoritative utterances, but as a factor in healing division, it takes significant place.

Amsterdam declared and demonstrated that the differences that lie in doctrinal statement and ecclesiastical practice are subordinate to and of lesser significance than the identities that lie in a common faith in Jesus Christ as God Incarnate and Saviour.

Amsterdam proved that men and women of many races and of many nations can worship, witness, and work together. True unity will emerge from such common experiences. Amsterdam established an organization through which Christians of the world may study, serve, speak, and stand together. Amsterdam recognized that within denominational differences precious truth is present, and that in the mutual sharing of spiritual possessions, all become richer and none poorer. A least common denominator, immediate *union,* would be of less value to the eventual union of the churches than the present preservation of the creative contributions of each denomination in the greatest common denominator, *unity,* now possible. There can be *union* without *unity,* and *unity* without *union.* It would appear that the road that leads to the churches becoming the Church is by way of the union of confessional families first. Then may come the reuniting of related confessions, and some day, please God, the Holy Catholic Church in which there is unity within union.

Amsterdam proved that intellectually honest men and women can pursue truth together in mutual respect, rejecting at once all attempts to coerce in the name of conformity or to control in the name of hierarchical authority. Within the conditions of freedom, relying upon democratic processes and rejecting any thought of super church or ecclesiastical totalitarianism, Amsterdam established a World Council of Churches. The basic unity of the individual church, free to express its convictions and to preserve its forms but bound to the law of love as revealed in Christ.

Amsterdam faced the baffling issues of international order and of economic and social organization realistically, and insisted that the church is obligated to give itself to those endeavors through which the moral law may come alive in the practices of the group life. All social systems are to be judged by the ethical ideals of the faith. Christians refuse to identify the Gospel with any economic theory or order.

Amsterdam created friendship and understanding, and in the hearts and minds of delegates are to be found the love and respect upon which the structure of the future will be reared.[2]

But the unity present is insufficient to meet the demands of over-all strategy. We must progress toward union. The need for unity is urgent. Time runs out. Our disunity is a denial of our Lord. It is disobedience of His command, disregard of His prayer. Disunity conceals the true nature of the Church. It must be evident to thoughtful Christians that we cannot win the world for Christ with the tactics of guerrilla warfare. We are not a resistance movement. We hold that Christ is to conquer, and that before His Name every knee shall bow. This calls for general staff, grand strategy, and army. And this means union.

Unfortunately, the very terms general staff, grand strategy, and army suggest a military organization, but the unity possible among Christians is one that will forever preclude the possibility of union upon the basis of autocratic organization. The democratic principle is essential. But there is no reason why upon the basis of democratically determined decision and the freedom inherent in the entire democratic concept, Christians cannot move as one.

We can no longer call upon God to bless us in wasting wealth and talent in useless duplication, not to say downright competition. Such inefficiency is sinful. We cannot preach with power when our consciences condemn the contradiction that lies in our proclamation of a Gospel that unites and our practice of a polity that divides. We dare not continue to impoverish our people by denying them the spiritual riches

[2] From article, "The Assembly and Practical Issues," in *Christendom.* Autumn, 1948.

possessed by other communions. We cannot proclaim and establish our dynamic common faith effectively as disorganized units when confronted by dynamic ideologies that move as one. Theism in a spiritual philosophy must be proclaimed by a united Church within the freedom of democracy, if mankind is to be saved from atheism and materialism promoted by totalitarian tyranny.

It is only a united, non-Roman Christianity that can hope to save Roman Christianity from its exclusiveness and its ecclesiastical totalitarianism, and thereby enable non-Roman Christianity and Roman Christianity to work together for the eventual unity of all Christendom and the building of Christ's Holy Church.[3]

To date, coöperation at the national and at the world level has been based upon a very simple formula, namely, the acceptance of Jesus Christ as Lord and Saviour or, as the World Council phrases it, as God and Saviour. Dr. Frederick M. Meek in "This Is The Church" insists "the experience which the believer has of Christ is primary." Dr. Charles C. Morrison holds that the basic requirement is the acceptance of "the sovereign Lordship of Christ." Dr. Meek added, "those who have shared in that experience are in truth the Body of Christ, seeking to do God's will. And wherever the Spirit of Christ is thus at work in a group of people, there is the church, and not a local church, but literally the church universal."

Is there not a truer basis for unity in the experience of the redeeming love of Christ and greater possibility of fellowship in the possession of the changed heart? How seldom does the word "love" appear in the historic formulations of faith? It is to be expected that a statement of faith will begin with the words, "I believe," but is there not an antecedent declaration in which we may find the words, "I love"? Much dis-

[3] From article, "Strategic Decisions, Not Tactical Details," in *Christendom*. Spring, 1948.

cussion in the realm of union is less an attempt to unite, growing out of loyalty to a common Lord, than to defend, emerging from insistences upon particular practices and particular statements of faith. It is somewhat disheartening to note the response of Canterbury to the union of the Church in South India. It was disappointing to face the fact that the plan for Episcopal and Presbyterian union in the United States was scuttled in the placid waters of Philadelphia. Responses to the proposals of the Congregational-Christian and Disciples of Christ in America, asking the Federal Council of the Churches of Christ in America to call a meeting of representatives of American Churches to consider "the possibility of immediate closer unity of American denominations which already accord one another mutual recognition of ministers and sacraments," ran the gamut from acceptances to refusals, not to mention an offer to "send observers." The recent decision in a lower court nullifying the attempts of the Congregational-Christian churches and of the Evangelical and Reformed Church to unite was disheartening.

Basically, we are one in a common loyalty to Jesus Christ, the Divine Lord and Saviour. In Him the Word became Flesh and dwelt among us. God was incarnate in Christ. Within the Church, the true seeker may find a consistent spiritual philosophy, unsurpassed moral teaching; full opportunity to express the life of the spirit in a life of service; and satisfying beauty in its services of worship—its music, its architecture. But antecedent to doctrine, morals, social service, and aesthetics, is the "pearl of great price," Jesus Christ, Himself, our Blessed Lord. It is He in Whom we have believed. It is He Who shall reign for ever and ever. It is upon the rock of this confession that the Church will be built.

If ten denominations in the United States whose membership approximates twenty millions were to make a great affirmative decision, namely, that we really want union and were to authorize representative commissions to meet, not to explore possibilities of union but to discover the means to give effect to the decision, I believe the way would be found. A church that calls for a united world must reveal the unity to which it summons the world, and plenipotentiaries should remain together long enough for a new Pentecost. The Holy Spirit was present in Jerusalem—He will be present in a conference that honestly strives for the reunion of Christendom. Representatives should be instructed not to enter into long and interminable discussion whose fundamental object is to preserve a particular emphasis. The object should be to discover together in the Spirit of Christ the bases upon which the church might become the Church. Such representatives would be forced to consider such matters as Apostolic Succession, immersion, ritual, episcopacy, second blessing, ruling elders, and much more. But if the grand decision had been made, it is not at all unlikely that the lesser factors which now divide would take their subordinate role. These factors may be preserved in unity. Unity does not emerge from them.

Too many of our previous attempts have been like meetings of the Security Council where each nation threatens veto.

The Church universal is divided into many churches; among them are the Protestant churches, the eastern Orthodox churches, the Roman Catholic church. In nearly all of them the Apostles Creed with its declaration, "I believe . . . in the Holy Catholic Church" is repeated in services of worship. No one of these churches to the exclusion of the others, is *the* Holy Catholic Church. All of them are parts of the Holy Catholic Church. The union of Christendom can never be achieved by one part of the Holy Catholic Church insisting that all other parts shall deny their Christian convictions in order to return to a part of the Church universal. Since the Roman Catholic church refuses at present to consider union except upon the basis of all other churches repudiating their own churches and returning to Rome, and since this exclusiveness, which refuses even to share in coöperative religious services, is both a denial of true catholicity and of the Spirit of Jesus, first steps toward union must be taken by the Protestant communions. The Protestant churches must continue the present brotherly and inspiring coöperation with the eastern Orthodox churches until such time as Protestantism is united and may then consider union with eastern Orthodoxy. When the full union of Protestantism and eastern Orthodoxy is accomplished and the Christians of the world belong to but two great churches, the leadership of that day may be Christian enough and creative enough to kneel before a common altar, beg forgiveness of the Christ for disunity and, sharing in the Bread and Wine of Holy Communion, rise in His Spirit to form the Holy Catholic Church to which all Christians belong.

That the reunion of the churches will involve constitution and proper provision for legislation, judicial decision and executive responsibility is self evident. That the world Church must be capable of acting at all levels from the world to the local church is likewise apparent. The structure requisite to the united Church can be designed. The problem is to become imbued with the Spirit essential to such designing, subsequent construction and continuous use.

Does it mean that all of us would be called upon to use the Prayer Book? Not at all. But certainly the beauty and the worth of the Prayer Book would soon be known. Such a conference might well arrange four or five Orders of Service for the United Church, and the local congregations might elect which service or services would be used. In the former Episcopal churches, of course the Prayer Book would continue, and among the Quakers, no doubt, the blessings of silence and the patient awaiting of the Inner Voice would continue, but as the years come and go, each would come to share in the riches of the other, and the services of worship preserving all the traditions of the centuries might become the possession of all.

Surely there would be little difficulty in choosing the name. The new Church would not be called The Methodist Church, nor the Baptist Church, nor the Presbyterian Church. Would we call it The Holy Catholic Church, or Christ's Holy Church?

Agreement is possible. Let the representatives be charged solemnly to keep their eyes upon the Christ rather than on the practices of a particular communion. He will be present, and where He abides there is the spirit of unity. We can preserve the precious forms of worship.

There can be a common ministry. It might call for a nation-wide sacred service of re-ordination or re-consecration in which the hands of the ministers of the different spiritual traditions might be laid upon the heads of all, and thereby each minister be blessed by the gifts that lie in all, each minister holding fast to the truth that Christ is the Consecrator and that the hands are hands used by Him, ordaining to sacred calling. Personally, I would be proud to kneel at any altar and to have the hands of Harry Emerson Fosdick placed upon my head, symbolizing the passing of the freedom and the independence of the Baptist tradition to the new Church. Similarly, I would rejoice in receiving from Henry Sloane Coffin the treasures of his traditions. I would count it an honor to have the hands of my dear friend, Bishop Henry Knox Sherrill laid upon my head, symbolizing the unbroken traditions of the centuries. And so through the other communions, as all in turn participate, thus all becoming new ministers in Christ Jesus.

The Sacraments of Baptism and the Holy Communion might be administered according to the different rites, but with the passing of the years the practices would become similar and the blessings of each brought together for the blessings of all. There can be full freedom in the preservation of tradition.

There can be united action at once in many fields. Our foreign or overseas missions could become one. We could have a common hymnal. Perhaps the Methodists might teach their Episcopal friends how to sing! There could be a Protestant daily paper. With what strength we could take up the modern media of radio and of television, and use them both for the glory of God! Visual education would cease to be the sorry attempt of amateurs who enter a field calling for the highest art. A united Protestantism could summon the talents of the greatest artists of the earth, and from the screen would come the message of our Lord. There could be a united system of higher education, unitedly supported, in which we would train the lay leadership of our Church, the teachers for our colleges and universities, and, in united theological seminaries, the ministers of the Church.

The union of American Christianity would electrify the world and accelerate the trends toward union in every continent. I write as one who has experienced the fact of union. The experience of Methodists in a united church validates faith in the larger union.[4]

If our divisions are to be healed we must begin the healing process at once. An omnibus volume was published following the meeting of the World Council in Amsterdam. It was entitled "Man's Disorder and God's Design." It contained the preliminary papers and study that formed the basis of the discussions in the sectional meetings. In the sections, four great themes were considered. 1. The Universal Church and God's Design. 2. The Church's Witness to God's Design. 3. The Church and the Disorder of Society. 4. The Church and the International Disorder. The volume contained the re-

4 From article, "Strategic Decisions, Not Tactical Details," in *Christendom.* Spring, 1948.

ports of the sections and the pronouncements of the Assembly.

The Methodist Church purchased 25,000 copies and sent one to each minister. In addition, a Study Guide and Annotated Bibliography was prepared. The Study Guide sought to make clear to the minister the essential argument presented in the papers, to raise questions for discussion, and to point out the emphases that differed fundamentally from the evangelical witness of Methodism. The annotated bibliography recommended the great books on Our Faith in God, Our Faith in Christ, Our Faith in the Bible, Our Faith in Love, Our Faith in Prayer, Our Faith in Immortality, Our Faith in the Holy Spirit, Our Faith in the Kingdom of God. Hundreds of discussion groups were formed across the country. Ministers read the large volume together, discussed the arguments together, and came to a fuller understanding of the views held by religious leaders of other communions.

In similar fashion the minds of all communions must be prepared for the thinking of brothers whose confessional emphases differ from other brothers. The heart must be made ready for the transforming power of love. Those who hold that religion lies primarily in doctrinal statement must be alerted to the meaning of experience in the realm of religion. The personal knowledge of the love of God and of its transforming power in human life is creative. The Gospel of salvation from sin means not alone forgiveness of past sins, but a new relationship which brings the assurance of final victory over everything that comes between man and God. This new Life, born at the Cross, is at every stage the Gift of God. It is something done for us. It is, at the same time, something done in us. The place of conversion must be recognized. The personal relationship to God upon which a man enters when he lays his heart and mind open to divine love bears witness to its own reality in the consciousness of the individual. Until we are able to confirm what the Church declares to be true by an inward authority, we shall still lack secure anchorage. The Gospel offers to men the assurance of divine forgiveness, but it does something more. It awakens the passion for holiness or perfect goodness, for a life that is conformed in every part to the image of God.[5]

The ecumenical idea must come alive in the hamlet, the home, and the heart. Ecumenical concepts must be made vivid in the sacred services of the Church: for instance, in the sacrament of Holy Communion. When next a child receives communion and hears the words of the Invitation, "Ye that do truly and earnestly repent of your sins, and are in love and charity with your neighbor, draw near with faith," and after a time kneels at the altar, and the minister reads, "Lift up your hearts," and the little one senses the Presence, does the child see in the sacred symbols a broken Body and a Life given for us? Of course! He has been taught that the ultimate became intimate in Jesus. Christ is present, but does he also sense the presence of that unbroken and universal fellowship that is the Church? Has he been taught that Metropolitan Jacob in far-off Travancore, wearing a silken robe and an embroidered headdress will be repeating a similar ritual and the people will receive similar symbols; that at Canterbury, the very words will be read as the blessed Bread and Wine are received; that in Frankfurt, Martin Niemöller, a modern prisoner of the Lord, brings his people to communion just as in the lovely Lal Bagh church in Lucknow the girls of the Isabella Thoburn College receive communion with their distinguished President, Sara Chakko, kneeling beside them; and also, that in ancient Edessa in accordance with the practice of the Greek Church, the brilliant and devoted Metropolitan Panteleimon likewise shares in communion? The spirit necessary to the reunion of the churches can be brought to the

[5] *The Episcopal Address to the General Conference of The Methodist Church,* 1948, pp. 23-24.

child through a process of re-education whereby the Bread and Wine of Holy Communion speak of One who died long since and is present for evermore, and also reveal the presence of that innumerable company united in the fellowship divine that we call the Church.

Similarly, in grace before meals, new content can be put into the words "Our Father." Every child can become aware of the privations and the hunger of the children of the world when mother and father repeat the blessing and say, "Our Father."

III

The second principle in Christian strategy is: Regain touch with dominant realities.

The rise of the worker to power is a fact of first significance. The man who was once a slave, then a serf, and finally a man free to sell his labor where he pleased, but actually exploited, has now, under democracy, moved to new status. He possesses new power. Great decisions made by the workers of the world are changing the course of history. This is a reality that the Church must face.

It does little good to send an occasional fraternal delegate to a central labor council, there to invoke the divine blessing. One great communion has determined to regain touch with reality by recruiting fifty of its ablest students each year. These students are to be individuals of vital religious experience, of commanding personality, of superior intellect. They are to pledge themselves to enter the labor movement and spend their lives in the movement, serving it, but more, bringing to it both the Spirit and the teachings of Christ. The Church plans to recruit these young people in the sophomore year, to urge upon them the broadest possible cultural preparation and then to send them to graduate study where they may be equipped in political science, in economics, in labor relations as well as further grounded in the Christian faith so that they are intellectually capable of presenting it to the most ardent Marxist.

Upon graduation, what are these students to do? To offer themselves as labor leaders? Not at all. They are to go to work —an unpaid missionary force earning their own living as miners, mechanics, road-builders, locomotive engineers. They are to join the labor organizations and as Christians to rise to such positions as their leadership and ability may justify. It is believed that within twenty years a thousand such young people will rise to local, state and national leadership. Christians will occupy the dominant positions in the labor movement.

There is no attempt to infiltrate. The Church asks nothing for itself. It is not an attempt to control the labor movement, directly or indirectly. It is an attempt through personality to bring the Christian philosophy to the place of decision. It is no attempt to tone down the demand for justice. As a matter of fact, individuals who will give themselves to such service, who refuse the invitations of management to higher positions and who are determined to remain with labor through the years are persons who will reject the compromises of expediency, and stand for principle in the hour of difficult decision. This plan is an attempt to regain touch with dominant reality in such fashion that Christ becomes Lord.

Theological education of the day trains men to meet the claims of other religions, but seldom equips the young minister to meet the challenge of dynamic ideologies such as Communism and Fascism. The Church must regain touch with dominant realities and so thoroughly understand Marxism that it may be in a position to meet its materialism, its theory of social development, its economics, and its advocacy of dictatorship, with a gospel so dynamic that thoughtful men may

see that the promise of reaching righteousness and brotherhood, justice and fraternity, lies in the freeing truth of this
faith rather than in the shackling falsities of Marx.

Following the Amsterdam meeting I preached one evening
at Central Hall, Westminster. Dr. W. E. Sangster, the brilliant and dedicated leader of that great enterprise, related an
amazing incident. He said, "One day just after Dunkirk a
representative of government phoned and asked if they might
have the use of the hall upon a Saturday morning." It is a
great auditorium seating nearly three thousand. The United
Nations held its first session there. Dr. Sangster continued,
"I had to refuse the request because we were going to have a
concert for children that morning. Then two members of the
cabinet came over to see me. They said, 'We are having trouble
getting out the coal. The Prime Minister is of the opinion if
he could speak to the coal-miners, the actual leaders from the
pits and put the whole situation up to them it might be
helpful.' " Dr. Sangster said, "I consented immediately. They
threw a cordon of soldiers around the church Friday night
and only the miners were allowed to enter. The coal-miners
came by plane and bus and train and early on Saturday morning three thousand of them were present.

"The Prime Minister rose and said, 'I want to give it to
you straight. You know after Dunkirk we had nothing. I
give it to you straight. Nothing. Two hundred guns, no
more; 20 tanks, that's all. I heard he was coming with a
million men—he referred to Hitler as he—and I said to
meself, the British navy will put 500,000 of them to the bot-
tom of the Channel, but what will we do with half a million
of them ashore?' He then went on for an hour and forty
minutes and outlined the desperate situation confronting
Britain. He came at last to a peroration, unequalled, I fancy,
in the oratory of Britain. He said, 'When at last it's over,
we'll parade these streets again. And as you go by, the people

will call out, And where were you? Someone will answer, I marched with the 8th Army, and someone else will say, I was in the skies over Britain. Another will reply, I was in the merchant marine pushing the ships through the sea up to Archangel. 'Then,' said Churchill, 'I shall be standing there and I shall see you marching by, the coal-miners of Britain, and I will call out, Where were you? And I will hear you answer, We were down in the black of the pits right up against the face of the coal.' " Dr. Sangster, with a voice full of emotion said, "Three thousand British coal-miners rose and with tears streaming down their faces cheered the Prime Minister—and the coal came out." The Church must get right up against the face of the coal! Right up against the face of the coal when it deals with the problem of hunger round the world; right up against the face of the coal when it meets the issues of injustice and of discrimination at home. The face of the coal is in the community in which we live, in our families, in ourselves.

It was for reasons such as these that Amsterdam in the much discussed report entitled "The Church and the Disorder of Society" said:

In the industrial revolution economic activity was freed from previous social controls and outgrew its modest place in human life. It created the vast network of financial, commercial and industrial relations which we know as the capitalist order. In all parts of the world new controls have in various degrees been put upon the free play of economic forces, but there are economic necessities which no political system can afford to defy. In our days, for instance, the need for stability in the value of money, for creation of capital and for incentives in production, is inescapable and world-wide. Justice, however, demands that economic activities be subordinated to social ends. It is intolerable that vast millions of people be exposed to insecurity, hunger, and frustration by periodic inflation or depression.

The Church cannot resolve the debate between those who feel that the primary solution is to socialise the means of production, and those who fear that such a course will merely lead to new and inordinate combinations of political and economic power, culminating finally in an omnicompetent State. In the light of the Christian understanding of man we must, however, say to the advocates of socialisation that the institution of property is not the root of the corruption of human nature. We must equally say to the defenders of existing property relations that ownership is not an unconditional right; it must, therefore, be preserved, curtailed or distributed in accordance with the requirements of justice.

On the one hand, we must vindicate the supremacy of persons over purely technical considerations by subordinating all economic processes and cherished rights to the needs of the community as a whole. On the other hand, we must preserve the possibility of a satisfying life for "little men in big societies." We must prevent abuse of authority and keep open as wide a sphere as possible in which men can have direct and responsible relations with each other as persons.

Coherent and purposeful ordering of society has now become a major necessity. Here governments have responsibilities which they must not shirk. But centres of initiative in economic life must be so encouraged as to avoid placing too great a burden upon centralised judgment and decision. To achieve religious, cultural, economic, social and other ends it is of vital importance that society should have a rich variety of smaller forms of community, in local government, within industrial organisations, including trade unions, through the development of public corporations and through voluntary associations. By such means it is possible to prevent an undue centralisation of power in modern technically organised communities, and thus escape the perils of tyranny while avoiding the dangers of anarchy.

The practice of segregation based upon color is a flagrant denial of the Christian teaching of the worth of personality and the fact of brotherhood. The Federal Council of the

Churches of Christ in America properly condemned the pattern of segregation and called for its elimination first in the Church. Marian Anderson was denied the right to sing in Constitution Hall, not because she lacked artistic ability, not because there was anything against her character, but because of her color. She is one of the great artists of the world, a Christian lady. Americans better acquainted with the Declaration of Independence and the traditions of this free land, Christians whose faith was more vital, men and women from both north and south, met the refusal at the Constitution Hall with an invitation to the Lincoln Memorial. Marian Anderson stood at last before a vast throng, black against the white marble, and he sat there—speaking still of government of the people, by the people, and for the people. She sang, "My Country 'Tis of Thee" and finally, "Ave Maria." Hail Mary, a Jewish girl! Hail Mary, a black girl!

The Church must regain touch with dominant realities. No single fact is used with greater effect by the infiltrating Communist as he seeks to win the colored peoples of the far east than the failure of Christians and of democracy to practice its principles in the matter of race relations. The Church cannot preach brotherhood effectively and suffer segregation in its fellowship.

IV

In the third place the Church must speak effectively upon the subject of war, as well as build constructively in the interest of peace. Its common faith must become a common purpose that eventuates in a common act. The Church is taking this strategic service seriously. The Federal Council's Commission on a Just and Durable Peace, chaired by the distinguished John Foster Dulles, exercised great influence at Dumbarton Oaks and particularly at San Francisco when the charter of the United Nations was adopted. The Methodist Crusade for a New World Order, and similar endeavors in other communions, were influential in changing the mood of the nation, which had been primarily isolationist or at least indifferent to internationalism, to a mood that demanded the creative participation of the United States in world affairs. Selfish nationalism gave way to sensible internationalism.

At Cambridge, England, in 1946 the Commission of the Churches on International Affairs was established. This commission recognized the necessity of competency in the presentation of principle to the great international bodies charged with decision. It was seen that the churches must be influential at the place decision is made before it is made. The membership of the commission is indicative of the seriousness with which the churches are facing this principle of strategy.

V

In many quarters the Church has been blind to the movement of God in history. Too often it has sided with vested interests of society and state and has failed to kindle the vision and purify the wills of men in a changing world.

Its fourth principle in grand strategy is: Behold God at work, summon Christians to take courage and to become co-workers with the Eternal.

For more than a century the churches of the world have sent missionaries to the far corners of the earth. In the name of a common Father they have taught the common man that every individual is a being of infinite worth. To the surprise of many, millions have believed, and the common man who has come to realize his worth calls for the freedom that is essential to the flowering of personality. The restless millions are no longer symbolized by Millet's famous peasants.

The amazing and revolutionary change wrought by God was perfectly and powerfully phrased by Edwin Markham. His "The Man with the Hoe," has become "The Man with a Hope."

THE MAN WITH THE HOE

Bowed by the weight of centuries he leans
Upon his hoe and gazes on the ground,
The emptiness of ages in his face,
And on his back the burden of the world.
Who made him dead to rapture and despair,
A thing that grieves not and that never hopes,
Stolid and stunned, a brother to the ox?
Who loosened and let down this brutal jaw?
Whose was the hand that slanted back this brow?
Whose breath blew out the light within this brain?

Is this the Thing the Lord God made and gave
To have dominion over sea and land;
To trace the stars and search the heavens for power;
To feel the passion of Eternity?
Is this the dream He dreamed who shaped the suns
And markt their ways upon the ancient deep?
Down all the caverns of Hell to their last gulf
There is no shape more terrible than this—
More tongued with cries against the world's blind greed—
More filled with signs and portents for the soul—
More packt with danger to the universe.

What gulfs between him and the seraphim?
Slave of the wheel of labor, what to him
Are Plato and the swing of Pleiades?
What the long reaches of the peaks of song,
The rift of dawn, the reddening of the rose?
Thru this dread shape the suffering ages look;
Time's tragedy is in that aching stoop;
Thru this dread shape humanity betrayed,

[127]

Plundered, profaned and disinherited,
Cries protest to the Powers that made the world,
A protest that is also prophecy.

O masters, lords and rulers in all lands,
Is this the handiwork you give to God,
This monstrous thing distorted and soul-quencht?
How will you ever straighten up this shape:
Touch it again with immortality;
Give back the upward looking and the light;
Rebuild in it the music and the dream;
Make right the immemorial infamies,
Perfidious wrongs, immedicable woes?

O masters, lords and rulers in all lands,
How will the future reckon with this Man?
How answer his brute question in that hour
When whirlwinds of rebellion shake all shores?
How will it be with kingdoms and with kings—
With those who shaped him to the thing he is—
When this dumb Terror shall rise to judge the world,
After the silence of the centuries?

THE MAN WITH A HOPE

I

Tyrants, the Tools begin to think;
And the long bondage, link by link,
Is breaking. Out of the ancient night
A new world rises, vast with might.
A star breaks on the chaos—lo,
The Shapes of the Dark begin to go!

II

Behold, O World, the Toiling Man,
Breaking at last the ancient ban,
Behold his brain!—so long his lack—

[128]

Must lift the burden from his back.
The hammers of thought within his brain
Must break at last the ancient chain.

For ages he has carried a curse
That darkened all his universe.
But after centuries of toil,
Ages that made his soul the spoil
Of tyrants and of traitors—see,
He ponders . . . and the world is free!

Hark, his world-shaking questions throng!
Thundering against the ancient wrong!
"Why am I bent with brutal loads?
Why driven an ox upon all roads?
Where is the laughter and the light
To cheer the workman in his might?
Why, since I feed the mouths of all,
Have I but the careless crumbs that fall?

Why with these labor-blasted hands
Am I left homeless in all lands?
Why is the one who builds the world
Left as a dog in the kennel curled?
Why is the one who beautifies
All Kingdoms, robbed of joyful eyes?
Why am I hurled thru hells of war,
I who have nothing to battle for?
Why called to cannon and battle blade,
To wreck the beauty I have made?
Why should I fight for lords, indeed,
I who have only mouths to feed—
I who am only the earth's old slave,
Whose only gain would be the grave?"

III

Behold, O World, the Toiler thinks!
Now these old questions of the Sphinx

[129]

Will have their answers. In this pause
Are epochs, institutions, laws—
The Fall of Anarchy and Chance—
The crumble of Brute Circumstance—
The building of the Comrade State,
To be a new benignant Fate—
The rise of Beauty to her throne,
To make all hearts her very own.

Chained to the earth the Toiler seems,
And yet his soul rides forth on dreams!
Tyrants, beware, for there is might
In dreams to shake the pillared night.
He ponders, and the moment awes;
For the world's fate is in that pause.
All the destinies are in that hush.
For in it is the power to crush
All the old battlements of wrong
And build the world in comrade song.
Ages the Night around him furled:
Behold the Morning of the World!

Princess Juliana, just before her coronation as Queen of
Holland, invited certain leaders of the World Council of
Churches to the palace for luncheon. Among them was Sara
Chakko, the president of the Isabella Thoburn College, in
Lucknow. She is a charming woman of splendid intellect and
great courage. She had come to Amsterdam glorying in the
fact that her people had won freedom. At the luncheon she
was given the seat at the right of Prince Bernard, and he,
trained in the way of princes, thought it his duty to set her
at ease and to make conversation. He did not know Miss
Chakko, knew nothing of her independence, was unaware
apparently of the pride in her heart as she thought of India
free. He said, "The situation in Indonesia gives us grave

concern." She turned and very quietly but compellingly said, "I should think it would."

There are some who do not see the Hand of God at work. They see the dark clouds of revolution. They are unaware that in such an hour God has given to men the high privilege of using freedom to establish justice, and thus to lead men to fraternity. If in ignorance, leaders fail to understand that God is at work and, like foolish Canute, seek to hold back the tides of social change they will be submerged. If men can see, in the restlessness of humanity, opportunity to lead and to serve, then tomorrow the deserts may bloom as the rose, and freedom be the lot of all men everywhere.

VI

In the fifth place, the Church must make it abundantly clear to all men everywhere that its interest is not in property, nor in power, nor in prestige. It refuses to summon men to a holy war. Its missionary enterprise is not for the purpose of furthering the foreign policies of states, nor the imperialistic designs, if such there be, of the powers of the west; its purpose is to teach the nations, baptizing them in the name of the Father and of the Son and of the Holy Spirit. It must be made clear to men everywhere that tyranny of every kind will be resisted by the Church. It must condemn as Amsterdam did: 1. Any attempt to limit the freedom of the Church to witness to its Lord in His design for mankind, and any attempt to impair the freedom of men to obey God and to act according to conscience, for those freedoms are implied in man's responsibility before God; 2. Any denial to man of an opportunity to participate in the shaping of society, for this is a duty implied in man's responsibility toward his neighbor; 3. Any attempt to prevent men from learning and spreading the truth. . . .

Amsterdam declared: "We denounce all forms of tyranny, economic, political, or religious, which deny liberty to men. We utterly oppose totalitarianism, wherever found, in which a state delegates to itself the right of determining men's thoughts and actions instead of recognizing the right of each individual to do God's will according to his conscience." Without qualification, the Assembly said, "We oppose aggressive imperialism—political, economic, or cultural—whereby a nation seeks to use other nations or peoples for its own ends."

Such declarations of grand strategy must be followed by action.

Strategy in the light of the world crisis was summed up in striking lines in the Assembly's message:

We have to learn afresh together to speak boldly in Christ's name both to those in power and to the people, to oppose terror, cruelty and race discrimination, to stand by the outcast, the prisoner and the refugee. We have to make of the Church in every place a voice for those who have no voice, and a home where every man will be at home. We have to learn afresh together what is the duty of the Christian man or woman in industry, in agriculture, in politics, in the professions and in the home. We have to ask God to teach us together to say "No" and to say "Yes" in truth. "No," to all that flouts the love of Christ, to every system, every programme and every person that treats any man as though he were an irresponsible thing or a means of profit, to the defenders of injustice in the name of order, to those who sow the seeds of war or urge war as inevitable; "Yes," to all that conforms to the love of Christ, to all who seek for justice, to the peacemakers, to all who hope, fight and suffer for the cause of man, to all who—even without knowing it—look for new heavens and a new earth wherein dwelleth righteousness.